BARRON'S

COMMON CORE SUCCESS
LEARN, REVIEW, APPLY

GRADE 6 ENGLISH LANGUAGE ARTS

what's your STORY

Erinn Hennessey

Consulting Editor

All inquiries should be addressed to:
Barron's Educational Series, Inc.
250 Wireless Boulevard
Hauppauge, NY 11788
www.barronseduc.com

ISBN: 978-1-4380-0679-6

Library of Congress Control Number: 2015932217

Date of Manufacture: June 2015
Manufactured by: C&C Offset Printing Co., Ltd, Shenzhen, China

Printed in China

9 8 7 6 5 4 3 2 1

As of August 2013, forty-six states and the District of Columbia had adopted the Common Core State Standards (CCSS) for English Language Arts (ELA) literacy and mathematics. These standards are geared toward preparing students for college, careers, and competition in the global economy. The adoption of the CCSS represents the first time that schools across the nation have had a common set of expectations for what students should know and be able to do. As with any new program, there are growing pains associated with implementation. Teachers are busy adapting classroom materials to meet the standards, and many parents are confused about what the standards mean for their children. As such, it is a prime opportunity for the creation of a workbook series that provides a clear-cut explanation of the standards coupled with effective lessons and activities tied to those standards.

The foundation of Barron's English Language Arts (ELA) literacy workbook for the sixth grade is based on sound educational practices coupled with parent-friendly explanations of the standards and interesting activities for students that meet those standards. While many other workbook series on the market today offer students practice with individual skills outlined in the CCSS, none seem to do so in a cohesive manner. Our goal was to create an exciting series that mirrors the way teachers actually teach in the classroom. Rather than random workbook pages that present each of the CCSS skills in isolation, our series presents the skills in interesting units of related materials that reinforce each of the standards in a meaningful way. We have included Stop and Think (Review/Understand/Discover) sections to assist parents/tutors and students in applying those skills at a higher level. The standards being addressed in each unit are clearly labeled and explained throughout so that parents/tutors have a better grasp of the purpose behind each activity. Additionally, sixth graders will be familiar and comfortable with the manner of presentation and learning as this is what they should be accustomed to in their everyday school experiences. These factors will not only assist students in mastering the skills of the standards for sixth grade, but will also provide an opportunity for parents to play a larger role in their children's overall education. Finally, the pedagogical stance of these workbooks will allow Barron's publishing to reach a wider audience. It is our view that it is not only parents and their children who will be able to use these books, but also tutors and teachers!

Lisa Wilson, M.Ed

Common Core Standards for English Language Arts

The following explanation of educational goals is based on Common Core English Language Arts standards that you child will learn in the sixth grade. A comprehensive list of the Common Core State Standards can be viewed at the following website: *www.corestandards.org*.

Understanding Standard Labels:

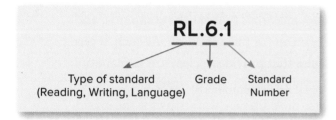

RL.6.1

Type of standard (Reading, Writing, Language) → Grade → Standard Number

Reading Standards
(RI: Reading Informational Text, RL: Reading Literature)

Key Ideas and Details
(Standards RI.6.1, RI.6.2, RI.6.3, RL.6.1, RL.6.2, and RL.6.3)

Your child will do/learn the following:

- Cite evidence from a text when analyzing what a text says explicitly and what can be inferred from the text
- Determine a theme or central idea of a text, explain how details support the theme or central idea, and summarize without using personal ideas or judgments
- Analyze how key individuals, events, or ideas are introduced and elaborated on in a text
- Explain relationships between people, events, and ideas in informational texts
- Describe how a plot unfolds and how characters respond as the plot moves toward a resolution

Craft and Structure
(Standards RI.6.4, RI.6.5, RI.6.6, RL.6.4, RL.6.5, and RL.6.6)

Your child will do/learn the following:

- Determine meanings of words and phrases, including figurative language and connotative meanings in texts
- Analyze how a sentence, chapter, scene, or stanza fits into the structure of a text and adds to the development of ideas, theme, setting, or plot
- Determine the author's point of view and how it is developed in the text or how the author develops the point of view of the narrator or speaker in a text

Integration of Knowledge and Ideas
(Standards RI.6.7, RI.6.8, RI.6.9, RL.6.7, and RL.6.9)

Your child will do/learn the following:

- Integrate information presented in different media or formats to develop an understanding of a topic or issue
- Evaluate the claim of an argument and distinguish between claims that are supported or not supported by reasons or evidence
- Compare and contrast one author's presentation of events with that of another
- Compare and contrast the experience of reading a story, drama, or poem to listening to or viewing an audio or video version
- Compare and contrast texts in different forms and genres in their approaches to similar themes and topics

Writing Standards (W)

Text Types and Purposes
(Standards W.6.1, W.6.2, and W.6.3)

Your child will do/learn the following:

- Write an argument (which includes introducing claims, supporting claims with reasons and evidence, using credible sources, using language to clarify relationships among claims and reasons, establishing and maintaining a formal style, and providing a conclusion)
- Write informative/explanatory essays (which includes introducing a topic, developing the topic with relevant information, using appropriate transitions, using precise language and domain-specific vocabulary, establishing and maintaining a formal style, and providing a conclusion)
- Write narrative essays (which includes developing a real or imagined experience or event, engaging the reader by establishing context and introducing a narrator or characters, organizing a natural and logical event sequence, using narrative techniques, using a variety of transitional elements to convey sequence and shifts in time, using details and sensory language to convey experiences and events, and providing a conclusion)

Production and Distribution of Writing
(Standards W.6.4, W.6.5, and W.6.6)

Your child will do/learn the following:

- Produce clear and coherent writing (argumentative essays, explanatory essays, and narrative essays) with appropriate organization and purpose
- Develop and strengthen writing by planning, revising, editing, and rewriting
- Use technology, including the Internet, to produce and publish writing

Research to Build and Present Knowledge
(Standards W.6.7, W.6.8, and W.6.9)

Your child will do/learn the following:

- Conduct research to investigate several sources to answer a question
- Gather information from a variety of sources, assess the credibility of the sources, quote or paraphrase information from the sources while avoiding plagiarism, and provide bibliographic information for sources
- Draw evidence from literary and informational texts to analyze, reflect, and research
- Apply reading standards for informational and literary texts to writing (for example, write a compare and contrast essay on literature characters or explain in writing how an author uses reasons and evidence to support a point)

Language Standards (L)

Conventions of Standard English
(Standards L.6.1.a–L.6.1.e, L.6.2.a, L.6.2.b)

Your child will do/learn the following:

- Correctly use pronouns, including using the proper case and intensive pronouns, and recognizing and correcting inappropriate shifts in pronouns and vague pronouns
- Recognize variation from standard English in their own or another's writing or speaking and identify and use strategies to improve conventional language
- Demonstrate command of the conventions of standard English capitalization, punctuation, and spelling when writing
- Use punctuation (commas, parentheses, dashes) to set off nonrestrictive elements
- Spell grade-appropriate words correctly

Knowledge of Language
(Standards L.6.3.a and L.6.3.b)

Your child will do/learn the following:

- Vary sentence patterns for meaning, reader interest, and style
- Maintain consistency in style and tone

Vocabulary Acquisition and Use
(Standards L.6.4.a–L.6.4.d and L.6.5.a–L.6.5.c)

Your child will do/learn the following:

- Use context clues to determine the meaning of a word
- Use Greek and Latin affixes and roots to determine the meaning of a word or phrase
- Use dictionaries and other reference materials to find the pronunciation and clarify word meaning or part of speech
- Verify word meaning by checking inferred meaning in context or in a dictionary
- Understand word relationships and interpret figurative language
- Use the relationships between words (cause/effect, item/category) to better understand those words
- Distinguish among connotations of words with similar denotations

Contents

Reading and Writing:
Informational Texts

Being able to read informational passages and understand their meaning is an important quality of a successful reader.

In this section, you will read a variety of historical and scientific material. The activities will test your ability to understand the information by asking you to answer questions based on what is directly stated as well as what may be only suggested in the texts.

Read the passage first so that you can pick out the main ideas. Look for other features such as the author's tone and point of view, as well as the organization of the passage itself. Refer back to the appropriate areas in the text as you work through each question. Using the evidence presented, sharpen your reasoning abilities by writing about what you've learned. Writing will help you to clarify new information by building upon what you know and what you feel to be true, or your opinion.

Happy reading and writing!

Wonders of the World

As people journeyed across the various countries of the world more than two thousand years ago, they recorded the amazing sights by drawing, writing, and collecting artifacts during their travels. In time, seven of these places made history and came to be called the Seven Wonders of the World. Today, other places have become world wonders. In this unit you will learn about a couple of them.

The Great Wall of China

1 Can you believe there is actually a wall that took over 1,700 years to build? It is the Great Wall of China. Over the course of history, various lists of world wonders have been created to record the world's most incredible natural and man-made structures. The Great Wall of China is one of these man-made wonders of the world, and it's easy to see why!

2 The building of this incredible wall began during the Warring States period of Chinese history under Emperor Qin Shi Huang, China's very first emperor, who ruled over 2,000 years ago between 220–206 B.C.E. This wall was built to protect and defend China's borders against attacks. Emperor Qin forced many people to work on the construction of the wall, including peasants, slaves, criminals, captured enemies, and even scholars. These people had little choice but to **submit** to his will. Ancient records show that many people died working to build the wall.

3 The work was exhausting, and the workers were not even paid! This early wall was built from local resources—earth and stones from the mountains.

4   While construction of the Great Wall began under the rule of Emperor Qin, not much of that wall still remains today. Most of what we see today was built under the **Ming Dynasty** from 1368 to 1644 C.E. During the Ming rule, China was attacked by various tribes, so the emperors decided to make the wall even better. They added to the existing wall and made it stronger. Like Emperor Qin before them, the Ming emperors forced many people to construct the wall. This time, the wall was made from bricks, limestone, and tiles. They built guard towers along the wall so that the guards could send smoke signals and fire cannons to warn of an attack. There are over 7,000 guard towers along the Great Wall, and it is estimated that over a million soldiers protected the wall during the Ming Dynasty.

5   While Westerners call the structure the "Great Wall of China," the Chinese call it the "Wan Li Chang Chen," which means the "Ten Thousand Li Long Wall." The *li* is a Chinese unit of length. The Great Wall brings a lot of tourism to the country. In fact, more than ten million people visit the wall each year. Tourists are usually stunned by the massive size of the wall when they see it in person. The wall is the longest man-made structure on earth and crosses the mountains of China for 4,500 miles. That's about 1,000 miles longer than the distance between New York and California.

6   The actual height and width of the wall varies from place to place, but it tends to be around twenty-five feet tall and fifteen to thirty feet wide, making it wide enough for two cars to drive on it! With its impressive size and unique history, it's clear why the Great Wall of China was named as one of the modern-day Seven Wonders of the World in 2007.

glossary

Submit: To accept or yield to the authority of another person.

Many people died during the building of the Great Wall because of unsafe working conditions, attacks from wild animals, and lack of food.

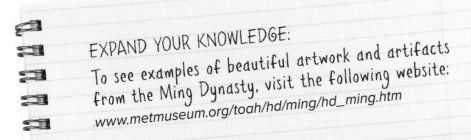

EXPAND YOUR KNOWLEDGE:
To see examples of beautiful artwork and artifacts from the Ming Dynasty, visit the following website:
www.metmuseum.org/toah/hd/ming/hd_ming.htm

CENTRAL IDEAS, KEY DETAILS, AND SUMMARIES

Use "The Great Wall of China" to answer the following questions.

Remember, the **central idea** is what the text is mostly about. The **key details** are different points from the text that connect to the central idea.

1. What is the **central idea** of the text?
   A. The Ming Dynasty built the Great Wall of China.
   B. The Great Wall of China is about 4,500 miles long.
   C. The Great Wall of China is a modern wonder of the world.
   D. There are over 7,000 guard towers along the Great Wall.

2. What **key details** from the text support the central idea?

   _____

   _____

   _____

   _____

3. Analyze the text and cite two of the most important concepts the author discussed when describing the Great Wall's history. Remember to use quotation marks around information cited from the text.

   _____

   _____

   _____

   _____

4. Explain why you think it was important for the author to first discuss Emperor Qin and then discuss the Ming Dynasty.

   _____

   _____

   _____

   _____

Standards RI.6.1, RI.6.2, RI.6.3

UNDERSTANDING VOCABULARY

Using context clues from the text, as well as reference materials, answer the following questions.

You can determine the meaning of an unknown word by looking at the surrounding words in the sentence. These are called **context clues**.

1. What does the term **submit** mean? Use clues from the passage to help you understand what this word means.

   _____

   _____

2. What was the **Ming Dynasty**? Use reference materials such as an encyclopedia or the Internet to find out.

   _____

   _____

   _____

SPELLING CORRECTLY

Even in the age of computer programs that check spelling, it is essential to learn how to correctly spell words on your own. Learning how to accurately spell words not only helps you become a better writer, but it also supports good reading skills.

One word in each of the following sentences is misspelled. Write the word correctly on the line.

1. The Great Wall of China is the longest man-made structer in the world.

   _____

2. The Great Wall of China reaches elavations of 5,000 feet above sea level.

   _____

3. The Great Wall of China is largely an acomplishment of the Ming Dynasty.

   _____

4. Tourists should use caushion when visiting the Great Wall because it is deteriorating.

   _____

5. The Great Wall of China is truly a wundrouss sight to see.

   _____

Stonehenge

1 Imagine finding a huge, circular **monument** made of giant stones sitting in the middle of a big open field. You might wonder who built it and why they built it. What purpose did it serve? Well, that's exactly what scientists have been wondering about a huge stone monument located in Wiltshire, England called Stonehenge.

Construction of Stonehenge

2 After studying this huge, mysterious monument for many years, **archaeologists** have learned a great deal about Stonehenge. The monument was built in stages, with the earliest part being built about 5,000 years ago. This means that Stonehenge is at least 300 years older than the earliest Egyptian pyramid! In the first phase of building, ancient people used primitive tools, such as deer antlers, to carve a massive, circular ditch and bank arrangement called a henge. Then, a few hundred years later, 80 bluestones were placed in a horseshoe shape at the center of the bank. This is what archaeologists call the inner circle of the monument. Bluestone is a type of volcanic rock, and the closest source of bluestone is located about 240 miles away from Stonehenge. Each of these bluestones weighs about four tons. It must have been quite a task for the ancient builders to move these stones over 240 miles during a time when the wheel had not even been invented yet! Today, only forty-three of these original bluestones remain standing. What archaeologists call the outer ring was built during the third phase of construction. The outer ring is made from sandstone slabs known as sarsen stones. These sarsen stones weigh up to forty tons each and stand about eighteen to twenty-four feet tall. Some of the sarsen stones were also arranged into three-piece structures called trilithons. No one really knows what methods the builders used to lift the huge stones onto the top of the trilithons. There are approximately fifty sarsen stones, but there may have been many more at one time.

Stonehenge is an ancient monument.

Trilithons at Stonehenge.

Who Built Stonehenge and Why?

3 There have been many theories suggested over the years about who built Stonehenge, but the fact is that no one really knows for sure. Some have said that ancient people called Druids built the monument to celebrate their religion, while others have claimed that aliens or even Merlin from the King Arthur legends built it. Right now, most archaeologists agree that several different tribes of people helped to build Stonehenge over a period of 1,500 years. Archaeologists are also not completely sure why it was built. Some theories include that this monument was a religious place of worship, a burial ground, or a solar observatory because it aligns with the midwinter and midsummer sunsets. We may never know the answers to these questions. However, with all of the mystery that surrounds Stonehenge, it's no surprise that it keeps people wondering!

CENTRAL IDEAS, KEY DETAILS, AND SUMMARIES

Use "Stonehenge" to answer the following questions.

1. **Summarize** the text in two or three sentences. In your summary, be sure to state the **central idea**, followed by **supporting details** from the text.

   _____

   _____

   _____

   _____

   _____

2. What are two important concepts the author discusses in the third paragraph?

   _____

   _____

3. In the text, the author introduces the idea that Stonehenge was built in stages. What evidence does he or she use to support that idea? Use quotation marks around information directly cited from the text.

   _____

   _____

   _____

EXPAND YOUR KNOWLEDGE:
To read more about the theories of who built Stonehenge and why, visit the following website:
http://ngm.nationalgeographic.com/2008/06/stonehenge/ alexander-text

Standards RI.6.1, RI.6.2, RI.6.3

ANALYZING STRUCTURE

The structure of a text affects how well you can understand it. Authors can add features such as titles, subheadings and photo captions to a text to make it more understandable. Some methods of structuring a text are chronological order, cause and effect, and compare/contrast.

Use "Stonehenge" to answer the following questions.

1. What two text features did the author of "Stonehenge" use when organizing this passage?

   _____

   _____

2. How does each of these text features help you as a reader?

   _____

   _____

3. What method does the author use for developing the ideas in the second paragraph?

   _____

   _____

UNDERSTANDING VOCABULARY

Using context clues from the text, as well as reference materials, answer the following questions.

1. What does the term **monument** mean? Use clues from the passage to help you understand what this word means.

   _____

   _____

2. What is an **archaeologist**? Use reference materials, such as an encyclopedia or the Internet, to find out.

   _____

   _____

UNIT 2

Celebrations of the World

People around the world celebrate many different occasions. These celebrations usually reflect the cultural and religious traditions of the country, and sometimes stem from ancient traditions practiced a long time ago. In this unit, you will learn about two world celebrations, how they came to be, and what they mean for the people today who observe them.

Chinese New Year

1 A story in Chinese legend says that a wild beast named *Nian*, which is also the word for "year," came out of the mountains at the end of each year to feast on humans. The only things that would scare the beast away were loud noises and bright lights. So, every year, the villagers would gather and use these methods to keep Nian away. This is how the Chinese New Year celebrations began. In modern-day China, the New Year celebration lasts for fifteen days and is filled with traditions, firecrackers, fireworks, and bright colors, particularly red. The Chinese use the lunar calendar for their festivals, so the date of the Chinese New Year changes every year. The date of the New Year celebration corresponds with the new moon in either late January or early February.

2 Leading up to the Chinese New Year celebrations, some very important traditions are observed. Houses are cleaned from top to bottom to sweep away all the bad luck of the previous year. Families often decorate the outsides of their homes with lights, and sometimes even give the front door and window panes a new coat of red paint. They also hang special decorations made from red and gold paper that are marked with messages of good fortune, such as the words "happiness" and "prosperity." Red and gold are the traditional colors because red is a lucky color thought to chase away the beast, Nian, and gold represents wealth.

Jiaozi are served at a traditional Chinese New Year's dinner.

3   During the Chinese New Year, there are many festivities. People get time off from work, and children sometimes get an entire month off from school! Families come together to celebrate. They gather for a traditional dinner, where *jiaozi* are usually served right before midnight. Jiaozi is a type of dumpling with a garlic-soy sauce. Often, a coin is hidden in one of these dumplings and is considered good luck to the person who finds it. Children receive *hong bao*, which are red envelopes containing money or sweets. There are also several street celebrations during the fifteen days of the Chinese New Year, including the Lion Dance, the Dragon Dance, and the Festival of Lanterns. In the Lion Dance, two dancers dress up as a lion, one acting as the head and the other as the body. A mirror is placed on the head of the lion so that bad spirits will be chased away when they see their own reflections. The lion dancers perform to drums, cymbals, and a gong. Dragon dances are also performed to scare away bad spirits. Many dancers participate in the Dragon Dance. The dragon costume can vary in length from just a few meters to up to 100 meters long. Dancers get under the costume and hold poles which raise and lower the dragon. Longer dragons are considered luckier than shorter ones. The Chinese New Year ends on the fifteenth day with the Festival of Lanterns. The streets are filled with music, dancing, and paper lanterns of all sizes. People paste riddles onto the lanterns so that others can guess at the answers. Lanterns are a Chinese tradition that is thought to bring good luck.

4   It is estimated that one out of every six people in the world participates in Chinese New Year celebrations. These celebrations occur all around the world, including China, as well as countries with high populations of Chinese people, such as Hong Kong, Taiwan, Singapore, Indonesia, and the Philippines. The celebrations also occur in locations around the world where "China Towns" are located, such as New York, NY and Los Angeles, CA. Wherever the celebration is held, it's likely to be bright, colorful, and filled with the traditions of family and wishes of good fortune.

CENTRAL IDEAS, KEY DETAILS, AND SUMMARIES

Use "Chinese New Year" to answer the following questions.

1. Choose the sentence that contains a fact-based **summary** of the text.
    A. The Dragon Dance only brings good luck if the dragon is long.
    B. The Chinese New Year celebration is colorful, cheerful, and fun.
    C. The Chinese New Year celebration is a yearly celebration involving many traditions.
    D. The Lion Dance is performed by two dancers to the sounds of drums, cymbals, and gongs.

2. Give three examples of the traditions celebrated using evidence from the text.

   _____

   _____

   _____

   _____

3. What evidence from the text supports the opinion that children love celebrating the Chinese New Year? Remember to use quotation marks when using a direct quote from the text.

_____

_____

_____

4. What influence does the legend of *Nian* still have on modern-day Chinese New Year celebrations?

_____

_____

_____

_____

EXPAND YOUR KNOWLEDGE:

In the Chinese zodiac, which follows a twelve-year cycle, each year is named after an animal. This tradition is based on a story in which the Jade Emperor invited all of the animals to a party, but only twelve showed up. As a reward, the emperor named a year after each one of them in the order in which they had arrived. According to tradition, depending on the year in which a person is born, he or she will have the character traits of the animal representing that year. To read about which Chinese animal represents the year you were born, visit the following website: http://kids.nationalgeographic.com/content/kids/en_US/explore/chinese-horoscopes/

REFLEXIVE AND INTENSIVE PRONOUNS

- Use reflexive pronouns to emphasize or intensify the subject of a sentence.
- It usually appears right after the subject (noun or pronoun) it is modifying.

> **List of Reflexive/ Intensive Pronouns:**
>
> | | | | |
> |---|---|---|---|
> | myself | himself | itself | yourselves |
> | yourself | herself | ourselves | themselves |

> Examples: I **myself** like to read mystery novels.
> (*Myself* is intensive and modifies *I*.)
>
> *Nian*, the beast, made **himself** an unwanted guest in the villages.
> (*Himself* is reflexive and modifies *Nian*.)

Use either an intensive or a reflexive pronoun to complete each of the following sentences. Label each with an (I) for intensive or an (R) for reflexive.

1. We _____ could not wait to see the Lion Dance at the parade! _____

2. James read to _____ about the traditions of the Chinese New Year. _____

3. Grandma _____ made the traditional dumplings for our dinner. _____

4. Our parents _____ cleaned our entire house for the New Year. _____

5. Anna bought _____ a red paper lantern for the Festival of Lanterns. _____

6. The Jade Emperor _____ named a year after each of the animals. _____

7. The dancers _____ made the elaborate lion costume for the dance. _____

8. I _____ am looking forward to receiving *hong bao* envelopes! _____

ACTIVE VOICE AND PASSIVE VOICE

Sentences are expressed in either active or passive voice.

Active voice presents things in a natural order and is usually more clear and direct. A **subject** (the "doer" or agent) performs an action or does something to an **object**.

Examples: The **cat** caught the **mouse**.   The **dog** buried his **bone**.
            subject   object   subject   object

Passive voice reverses the natural order. The object of the sentence is placed in the subject position and becomes the focus of the sentence. The problem is that this subject is still not the "doer" of the sentence. It is still being acted upon by another agent. Passive sentences tend to be longer and more confusing.

Examples: The **mouse** was caught by the **cat**.   The **bone** was buried by the **dog**.
            subject but   agent or   subject but   agent or
            not a "doer"   "doer"   not a "doer"   "doer"

The active voice is usually preferred in academic writing. If you use the active voice, your writing will be more clear and direct!

Rewrite the following paragraph so that all the sentences that use the passive voice are changed to the active voice.

In early China, the villages were attacked by Nian, a furious mountain beast, every month. A suggestion was made by a wise old man in the village to conquer the monster. Drums were beaten, red robes were worn, and firecrackers were thrown by villagers to frighten the beast. The Nian was scared away by these loud noises and bright lights for a year. The traditional lion dance is performed by modern Chinese people every year in New Year celebrations to honor the Chinese legend.

_____

_____

_____

_____

_____

_____

_____

_____

_____

_____

_____

Digging Deeper

To learn more about the history and traditions of the colorful festival known as Chinese New Year, view the video at the following website: *www.history.com/topics/holidays/chinese-new-year/videos*

Carnival in Rio de Janeiro

1 It is late February or early March. The streets are full of parades and floats. Dancers in bright, colorful costumes twirl to the rhythm of loud samba music. People are laughing and smiling everywhere you look. Where are you? You are in Rio de Janeiro, Brazil, for the largest party in the world!

2 While it's true that Carnival celebrations are held all over the world in places like Italy, France, England, Greece, Russia, and the United States, the Rio de Janeiro Carnival is the largest one in the world, according to the *Guinness Book of World Records*! Every day during Carnival, there are over two million people in the streets. In 2011 alone, 4.9 million people celebrated Carnival in Rio, and about 400,000 of them were foreigners who traveled to Brazil just to participate in the fun!

3 What is Carnival, and how did it start? Many people debate the actual history and dates of origin of the Rio de Janeiro Carnival. The festival itself is likely rooted in both non-Christian and Christian religious festivals. Ancient Greeks and Romans held festivals every year to celebrate the coming of spring. Later, these practices were adopted in Italy and became the basis of the famous Carnival in Venice. Eventually, Carnival celebrations became popular throughout Europe, and it is thought that the Portuguese brought Carnival to Brazil. These early Carnival celebrations were short periods of time when traditional rules of society were forgotten. Regular citizens would wear the clothing of royalty, while the rich would wear the clothing of the less fortunate, as they all paraded and danced in the streets. It was a time of equality and unity. The first official festivals in Rio date back to around 1723. Today, the Rio Carnival, like Mardi Gras in New Orleans and the Venice Carnival, takes place during the four days just before the start of the Christian celebration of Lent, a holy week to prepare for Easter.

4 During the 1800s, the practices of many groups became a part of Carnival tradition. Some of the original celebrations were luxurious parades held by aristocrats, street parades held by the working class, and masked costume parades held by the lower class. These all became part of the modern-day Carnival tradition. Another large influence on the Rio Carnival is African culture. Brazil's economy in the 1800s was largely based on slavery; the country alone held thirty-five percent of the world's slaves. The culture of the African slaves had a major impact on the celebrations of Carnival, especially in the form of music. Samba music, which is the music played during Carnival, originated from a blend of street music and slave songs. Samba music led to the creation of the samba dance. Today, the magnificent street parades of Carnival are filled with samba music and samba dancing.

5 Samba music and samba dancing became so popular that citizens began to compete against each other in samba competitions. This lead to the creation of what are called samba schools, where people gather and practice samba dance routines to perform during Carnival. Because of the popularity of these schools and the increased competition, the Sambadrome was built. It is a large building where huge crowds gather to watch the samba competition. During the last two days of the Carnival, the top twelve samba schools compete for the championship at the Sambadrome. This competition is broadcast live on television all over the nation of Brazil.

6 The world's largest party sure does sound like a lot of fun! From the unique sounds of samba music, to the colorful parades, to the energetic samba dancing, the Rio de Janeiro Carnival brings millions of people together to laugh, dance, and celebrate!

CENTRAL IDEAS, KEY DETAILS, AND SUMMARIES

Use "Carnival in Rio de Janeiro" to answer the following questions.

1. Which sentence provides a fact-based **summary** of the text?
   A. The Carnival in Rio is celebrated every year in late February or early March.
   B. The Carnival in Rio is a non-Christian festival that people enjoy celebrating each year.
   C. The Carnival in Rio includes many traditions and is the biggest party in the world.
   D. The Carnival in Rio thankfully provides a chance for equality for all people.

2. Write three details from the text that the author uses to support the **central idea**.

   _____

   _____

   _____

3. What evidence from the text supports the idea that the Rio de Janeiro Carnival is the largest party in the world?

_____

_____

4. What influence did African culture have on modern-day Rio de Janeiro Carnival celebrations?

_____

_____

_____

PRONOUN CASES

Pronouns display "case" depending on their function in a sentence. There are three cases.

- **Subjective**—The pronoun acts as the subject or "doer" of the sentence.

> Example: **She** took the dog for a walk.

- **Possessive**—The pronoun shows possession or ownership of something else.

> Example: Rover, the dog, waits patiently by the door with **his** leash.

- **Objective**—The pronoun receives the action of the sentence.

> Example: She tries to walk **him** every day.

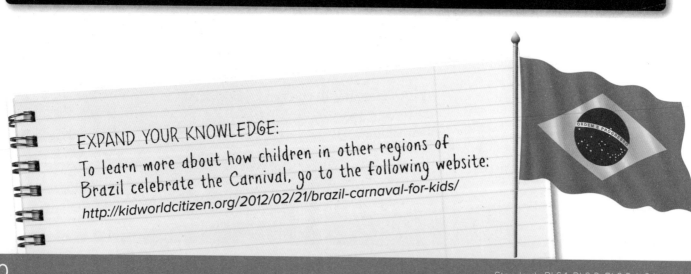

EXPAND YOUR KNOWLEDGE:
To learn more about how children in other regions of Brazil celebrate the Carnival, go to the following website:
http://kidworldcitizen.org/2012/02/21/brazil-carnaval-for-kids/

Standards RI.6.1, RI.6.2, RI.6.3, L.6.1.a

Costumed samba dancers participate in televised competitions during Carnival.

Read the following sentences and determine if the pronoun is in the subjective case (S), the possessive case (P), or the objective case (O).

1. _____ Cameron danced his heart out at the samba competition.

2. _____ Cameron's friends watched him compete in the samba competition on TV.

3. _____ He wanted to win the samba competition this year.

4. _____ The samba dancers quickly moved their feet to the beat of the music.

5. _____ The dancers waved to us as they passed on the way to the Sambadrome.

THE CASE OF "I" AND "ME"

- A pronoun's position in the sentence always determines which case should be used.
- Writers sometimes get mixed up when these pronouns are used with compound subjects or compound objects (when there is more than one subject or object).

> **Example:** Grandma asked Sarah and **me** to take out the trash. (objective case)
> Sarah and **I** took out the trash. (subjective case)

Hint: Read the sentence with only the pronoun to see if it makes sense.

> **Example:** Grandma asked Sarah and **I** to take out the trash. **(INCORRECT)**
> You would never say, "Grandma asked **I** to take out the trash."

Complete each of the following sentences with either the subjective case ("I") or objective case ("me").

1. Luis waved to Marco and _____ at the parade.

2. Tara and _____ are going to the biggest party in the world!

3. All that samba dancing practice left Angie and _____ very tired.

4. Sergio and _____ wanted to learn to play drums for the Carnival parade.

5. Hugo and _____ got lost in the huge crowds at the Carnival.

Digging Deeper

Visit the following website to hear a recording of samba music: *www.npr.org/player/v2/mediaPlayer.html?action= 1&t=1&islist=false&id=285299211&m=285840306*

WRITE YOUR EXPLANATION

After reading "Chinese New Year" and "Carnival in Rio de Janeiro," use the graphic organizer to plan a short, one-paragraph essay explaining the similarities and differences between these two celebrations. Before beginning the assignment, you may want to make a list of similarities and differences on a separate sheet of paper. Use textual evidence as supporting details. Remember to use quotation marks when using a direct quote from one of the passages.

Introduction (Topic sentence that states the main idea):

_____

_____

Similarity or Difference:

_____

_____

_____

Similarity or Difference:

_____

_____

_____

Similarity or Difference:

_____

_____

_____

Supporting Detail:

_____

_____

_____

_____

Supporting Detail:

_____

_____

_____

_____

Supporting Detail:

_____

_____

_____

_____

Conclusion (Concluding sentence that summarizes the main idea):

_____

_____

Ancient Civilizations of the World

In this unit, you will explore some of the most interesting civilizations that existed thousands of years ago. If you are passionate about history, you will enjoy reading about these advanced civilizations as you journey to discover these ancient worlds.

Fall of the Mayan Empire

1 Did you know that the Mayan civilization is one of the most mysterious civilizations in world history? The Mayan Empire, while centered in what is now modern-day Guatemala, actually covered all of the Yucatan Peninsula, Guatemala, Belize, parts of Mexico, and the western parts of Honduras and El Salvador. The Mayan Empire lasted for almost 3,000 years from about 1800 B.C. to around 900 C.E. and reached the peak of its power and influence around the sixth century C.E. This peak happened in what is called the Classic Period of the Mayan civilization from 250 to 900 C.E. Although the Mayan Empire was one of the most powerful societies in the region, a mysterious decline and collapse of their civilization occurred. There are many theories about how and why this happened, but it is likely that no single theory is the solution to the mystery.

Advanced Society

2 The Maya lived in a very advanced society. During the Classic Period, there were over forty cities in the empire, and the population was probably around 2,000,000. The Maya built many plazas, temples, pyramids, and courts for playing ball games in these cities. Many of these temples and plazas were built in a stepped pyramid shape and included **elaborate** decorations and inscriptions, or carved messages. The cities were supported by a large population of farmers who lived in the surrounding areas. The Maya were also advanced when it came to mathematics and astronomy. They observed and recorded objects, such as planets and stars in the night sky, and lined their giant temples up precisely with these objects.

3 They also accurately predicted things, like lunar and solar eclipses, and even developed a complex calendar system based on a 365-day cycle. Does that sound familiar?

4 The Maya participated in trade as well, especially with valuable items like jade and obsidian, which are both beautiful stones. They made paper from tree bark and wrote books using their own system of **hieroglyphic** writing.

Collapse

5 So, how could a society this advanced suddenly disappear? That's a question that experts have been working to answer for a long time. Exploration

> ### glossary
>
> **Elaborate:** Complex, full of detail, or ornate.
>
> **Hieroglyphics:** A form of writing which uses pictures or symbols to represent objects or concepts.

Map of Mayan Empire.

of the Mayan ruins began around 1830, and what we know of this ancient civilization comes from the study of what has been found at the sites of the former Mayan cities. Based on hieroglyphs and pictures found at many sites, experts believe that the Mayan civilization was doing very well until about 904 C.E. when suddenly, all the writing and signs of an active society stopped. Experts have come up with several theories to explain the disappearance of this once-mighty empire. However, it is likely that no single theory holds the answer. A combination of these factors is probably what shook the foundation of the Mayan civilization and brought it to its knees.

The Theories

6   Theory 1: The first theory that explains the collapse of the Mayan Empire is that some sort of disaster occurred. Some experts believe that a long, intense drought, a volcanic eruption, an earthquake, or an epidemic disease could have doomed the civilization.

7   Theory 2: A second theory that explains the collapse of the Mayan Empire is that there was not enough food being produced on the farms to support the large growth in population in the cities. It is possible that the Maya also overused the land to keep up with food production. If a large farming problem, such as a drought or plant disease occurred, it would definitely have doomed the civilization already struggling to feed itself.

8   Theory 3: A third theory that explains the collapse of the Mayan Empire is that there was unrest among the people. Experts know that the Maya went to war with each other all the time. This would have created many military and economic issues. Adding to those problems was the possibility that as the populations grew, the working class people who grew the food, built the temples, and mined the jade and obsidian would have been placed under greater strain to work harder. The problem would have been even worse if food was scarce. It is possible that an overworked working class may have overthrown the ruling class of citizens.

Conclusion

9   It is more than likely that no single theory is correct and that some combination of the three theories is what led to the collapse of the Mayan Empire. It would be nearly impossible for any single factor to cause the almost immediate collapse of an entire powerful empire. Overpopulation, overuse of land, warfare among the Mayan cities, and natural disasters probably all played a role in the mysterious disappearance of the once-mighty civilization of the Maya.

EXPAND YOUR KNOWLEDGE:
The Mayan people developed a complex and accurate calendar system to track agricultural and ceremonial cycles. To learn more about the Mayan calendar and how it works, visit the following website:
http://maya.nmai.si.edu/

CENTRAL IDEAS, KEY DETAILS, AND SUMMARIES

Use "Fall of the Mayan Empire" to answer the following question.

1. Which statement best reflects the **central idea** of the text?
    A. There are many theories about why the powerful, ancient Mayan Empire collapsed.
    B. There were many math and astronomy advancements made by the Mayan Empire.
    C. The peak of the Mayan Empire, called the Classic Period, was from 250 to 900 C.E.
    D. The mysterious collapse of the Mayan Empire happened somewhere near 900 C.E.

DETERMINING POINT OF VIEW AND PURPOSE

Point of View—This is an author's expressed opinion or view on a topic within a text.

Purpose—The reason why a text was written. The three purposes are as follows:

-   To inform (or teach)
-   To persuade (or convince)
-   To entertain

1. Which best states the **author's purpose** for writing the passage?
    A. To entertain readers with information on the Mayan Empire
    B. To persuade readers about the advancements of the Mayan Empire
    C. To teach readers about the culture and collapse of the Mayan Empire
    D. To inform readers about the people and art of the Mayan Empire

2. Which sentence best states the author's **point of view** in the passage?
    A. The first theory that explains the collapse of the Mayan Empire is that some sort of disaster occurred.
    B. There are many theories about how and why this happened, but it is likely that no single theory is the solution to the mystery.
    C. While the Mayan Empire was one of the most powerful societies in the region, a mysterious decline and collapse of their civilization occurred.
    D. It is possible that an overworked working class may have overthrown the ruling class of citizens.

ANALYZING STRUCTURE

Use "Fall of the Mayan Empire" to answer the following questions.

For a reminder of the different types of text features, refer back to page 19.

1. What text features did the author of "Fall of the Mayan Empire" use?

   _____

2. Choose one of these text features and explain how it helped you as a reader.

   _____

   _____

3. What purpose does the second paragraph serve in the rest of the passage?

   _____

   _____

4. Why is the first sentence in the conclusion especially important?

   _____

   _____

EVALUATING AN ARGUMENT

1. What **claim** does the author make about the collapse of the Mayan Empire?

   _____

2. Which sentence makes a claim that is **not** supported by information in the text?
   A. Warfare amongst the Mayans made the civilization weaker.
   B. A volcanic eruption or earthquake may have affected the Mayans.
   C. The Mayans had an advanced society, especially in the Classic Period.
   D. Climate change affected Mayan farming, fishing, and hunting.

Digging Deeper

Archaeologists have discovered a previously unknown part of Mayan civilization in the Yucatan Peninsula of southern Mexico. To watch a video about this discovery and about the collapse of the Mayan Empire, visit this website:
http://video.pbs.org/video/2216399796/

UNDERSTANDING VOCABULARY

Understanding word meanings and the meanings of common phrases helps you comprehend what a text is trying to tell you. You can use reference materials, such as dictionaries, encyclopedias, and the Internet, to clarify vocabulary. Using other clues, such as analogies or word relationships, can help you understand words with the same meanings.

Use "Fall of the Mayan Empire" to answer the following questions.

1. What does the author mean by the phrase "**brought it to its knees**" in the following sentence?

   *"A combination of these factors is probably what shook the foundation of the Mayan civilization and **brought it to its knees**."*

   _____

   _____

2. What is the meaning of **elaborate** in the following sentence?

   *"Many of these temples and plazas were built in a stepped pyramid shape and included **elaborate** decorations and inscriptions, or carved messages."*

   A. generous or kind

   B. detailed or complicated

   C. plain or dull

   D. attractive or beautiful

ANALOGIES

Analogies are two pairs of words that share similar, logical relationships. To understand an analogy, you must first form a logical relationship between two words. Then, you need to recognize when another pair of words has that same relationship.

> Examples: "**Green** is to **grass** as **blue** is to **sky**."
> "**Lace** is to **shoe** as **zipper** is to **jacket**."

Circle the word in parentheses that best completes each analogy.

1. Glyphs are to symbols as letters are to (words / books).

2. Silver is to metal as jade is to (valuable/stone).

3. Build is to rise as (wreck /collapse) is to fall.

4. Peninsula is to land as (thumb / knuckle) is to hand.

Decline of the Egyptian Empire

1   The pyramids, the Sphinx, pharaohs, and mummies are probably things that come to mind when you think about ancient Egypt. While it's true that all of these things were part of ancient Egyptian culture, there was so much more to it than that. The ancient Egyptian Empire was probably the most advanced and culturally-rich civilization the world has ever known. It lasted for over 3,000 years and was an ancient superpower. How could such an advanced, powerful empire come to an end? While there is no single factor that caused the **decline** of the empire, it seems that several things that occurred over hundreds of years had long-lasting effects, and eventually led to the fall. These included economic issues, military issues, and religious issues.

Rise of an Empire

2   Two major kingdoms called *Upper Egypt* and *Lower Egypt* developed along the Nile River around 5500 B.C.E. One ruler, King Narmer, brought both kingdoms together around 3200 B.C.E. This marked the beginning of what we call Egyptian civilization. King Narmer built the capital of ancient Egypt on the border between Upper and Lower Egypt and named the city Memphis. The Egyptian king, or pharaoh, was the absolute ruler and owned just about everything in the kingdom, including the people! In fact, the Egyptian people believed the pharaoh was a living god. The first pharaohs of Egypt established a dynasty, or family control of the government. In all of the Egyptian Empire, there were around thirty different dynasties. The history of the Egyptian Empire is divided into three major periods: the Old Kingdom, the Middle Kingdom, and the New Kingdom. It is important to understand some of the events that occurred in these periods to then understand why the empire eventually fell.

Egyptian Timeline

3   During the Old Kingdom, which lasted from about 2700 B.C.E. to 2200 B.C.E., the Egyptians built the Great Sphinx, as well as the now famous pyramids at Giza as tombs for their pharaohs. Sometime during the end of the Old Kingdom and the beginning of the

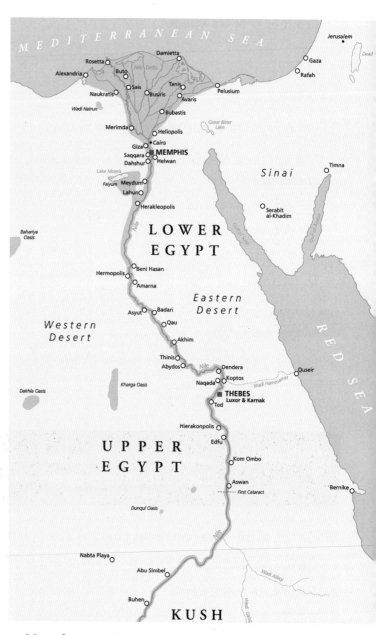

Map of ancient Egypt.

Middle Kingdom, there was a series of civil wars among the people, and Egypt was ruled by many local leaders. The Egyptian society was sharply divided between the richer ruling classes and the working poorer classes. Around 2050 B.C.E., a new king united Egypt again, and moved the capital from Memphis to Thebes. The Middle Kingdom pharaohs were less powerful than the Old Kingdom pharaohs.

4   Toward the end of the Middle Kingdom, a civil war amongst the Egyptians broke out again, and there was an invasion by people from the north called the Hyksos. The Hyksos conquered Egypt and ruled for about 100 years. The Egyptian people did not like the Hyksos at all and were finally able to overthrow them. This marked the beginning of the New Kingdom at around 1560 B.C.E.

5   It was under the New Kingdom pharaohs that the wealth, power, and territory of the Egyptian Empire grew dramatically. This expansion required a large Egyptian military. It was also during the New Kingdom that some of Egypt's most famous pharaohs ruled. During the New Kingdom, a pharaoh named Akhenaten completely changed the religion in Egypt. Instead of worshipping many gods, they were now only to worship the sun god, Aten. This angered the powerful religious leaders and caused citizens to be confused and upset. Akhenaten also moved the capital city from Thebes to a place called Tel-El-Amarna. When Akhenaten's son, Tutankhamun, or King Tut, became king, he **reversed** the changes his father had made to the religion. It was also during the New Kingdom that the Ramses Dynasty ruled. In fact, one of Egypt's greatest pharaohs was Ramses II, or Ramses the Great. Eventually, around 945 B.C.E., Egypt was conquered and ruled by several different foreign powers, including the Persians, the Greeks, and the Romans.

Sphinx and pyramids at Giza.

glossary

Decline: A gradual worsening in condition or quality.

Reverse: To make something the opposite of what it was.

Old Kingdom

- United Egypt
- Building of pyramids of Giza and Sphinx
- Civil wars at end of Old Kingdom

Middle Kingdom

- Pharaohs less powerful
- Civil wars and invasion of Hyksos at end of Middle Kingdom

New Kingdom

- Rule of Akhenaten Ramses Dynasty
- Conquered and ruled by foreign powers at end of New Kingdom

The Fall of an Empire

6   It is impossible to point to a single event or thing that caused the decline and fall of the once powerful Egyptian Empire. However, some of the key factors that most definitely played a part in the eventual collapse were economic issues, military issues, and religious issues. First, there was a great divide between the rich and the poor in Egyptian society. The rich, including the pharaoh and religious leaders, were the ruling class who controlled everything. The religious leaders even owned thirty percent of the nation's land! This likely led to many of the internal or civil wars in Egypt, which only weakened the empire. Second, ruling and expanding a large empire costs a lot of money because more soldiers and equipment are needed. For example, Pharaoh Ramses III led Egypt to war during the New Kingdom to conquer Syria, and this was very expensive. The cost of maintaining such a huge empire likely weakened the Egyptian economy. Finally, since religion was a major part of Egyptian life, the actions of Pharaoh Akhenaten in completely replacing the old religion caused a big problem. Even though Akhenaten's son, King Tut, changed everything back to the way it had been before, the society never completely healed from the damage. No single thing caused the collapse of the once-mighty Egyptian Empire, but a series of events and cultural practices did.

EXPAND YOUR KNOWLEDGE:
Visit the following website to learn all about the amazing writing system called hieroglyphics used by the ancient Egyptians:
http://history-world.org/hieroglyphics.htm

CENTRAL IDEAS, KEY DETAILS, AND SUMMARIES

Use "Decline of the Egyptian Empire" to answer the following questions.

1. **Summarize** the **central idea** of the text. Be sure to include details from the text to support the central idea.

_____

_____

_____

_____

_____

_____

_____

DETERMINING POINT OF VIEW AND PURPOSE

1. Which of the three main purposes for writing best describes the **author's purpose** for writing the text?

_____

_____

_____

_____

_____

Remember, a text can be written to inform (or teach), to persuade (or convince), or to entertain.

2. Which sentence best states the author's **point of view** in the passage?
   A. The Middle Kingdom pharaohs caused the collapse of the Egyptian Empire.
   B. A bad economy and warfare led to the decline of the Egyptian Empire.
   C. Constant civil wars led to the decline and collapse of the Egyptian Empire.
   D. Several factors led to the decline and collapse of the Egyptian Empire.

EVALUATING AN ARGUMENT

Understanding and following the logic of an argument an author is trying to make will deepen your reading comprehension.

Use "Decline of the Egyptian Empire" to answer the following questions.

1. What **claim** does the author make about the decline of the Egyptian Empire?

   _____

   _____

   _____

   _____

2. List the supporting details the author uses to support his or her claim.

   _____

   _____

   _____

   _____

   _____

   _____

3. Which sentence makes a claim that is **not** supported by information in the text?
   A. The Egyptian Empire reached its peak during the New Kingdom.
   B. Pharaoh Akhenaten disrupted the kingdom and changed the religion.
   C. The Egyptian Empire grew powerful under the rule of the Hyksos.
   D. The most famous Egyptian structures are from the Old Kingdom.

Digging Deeper

Have you ever wanted to see the Sphinx and pyramids up close? Explore the Sphinx and the Great Pyramid of Giza on this interactive website: *www.pbs.org/wgbh/nova/ancient/explore-ancient-egypt.html*

UNDERSTANDING VOCABULARY

Use "Decline of the Egyptian Empire" to answer the following questions.

1. What is the meaning of **reversed** in the following sentence?

   *"When Akhenaten's son, King Tut, became king, he **reversed** the changes his father had made to the religion."*

   _____

2. What is the meaning of **decline** in the following sentence?

   *"While there is no single factor that caused the **decline** of the empire, it seems that several things that occurred over hundreds of years had long-lasting effects, and eventually led to the fall."*

   _____

ANALOGIES

Circle the word in parentheses that best completes each analogy.

1. Queen is to England as (pharaoh / empire) is to Egypt.
2. Win is to lose as (yield / conquer) is to surrender.
3. Rich is to (wealthy / poverty) as poor is to needy.

WRITE YOUR EXPLANATION

Compare and contrast the fall of the Mayan and Egyptian empires. Use the Venn diagram to list the similarities and differences you see between the two empires. Remember to include transition words and to use domain-specific vocabulary.

Fall of the Mayan Empire

Same

Fall of the Egyptian Empire

Write a short, one-paragraph essay that compares and contrasts the fall of each of these great civilizations. Use the details you collected on the Venn diagram along with the following outline to guide your writing, and list some details or examples from the text for support.

- Introduction—Introduce the topic of comparing and contrasting the fall of the empires. List the points of comparison you will use (for example: economy, religion, food sources, etc.).

- Write about a few similarities between the two empires.

- Write about a few differences between the two empires.

- Conclusion—Restate that the essay was a comparison between the two empires and the points upon which you based your comparison.

Congratulations! You have completed the lessons in this section. Now you will have the chance to practice some of the skills you just learned.

Collapse of the Roman Empire

1   Many of the things in our culture come straight from the ancient Roman Empire. Right now, you are reading words on a page, and those words are made from letters. Those letters come right from the alphabet created by the Romans thousands of years ago! While you are in school, if you learn that Latin root words and affixes are used in the English language, you can thank the Romans because Latin was the Roman language! The Roman Empire was one of the greatest civilizations ever known, and its culture still has a large impact on our world today, especially in areas

The Roman Empire
in 117 AD, at its greatest extent

such as language, literature, architecture, and government. This empire conquered the regions we now know as England and Wales, Spain, France, Greece, the Middle East, and the Northern African coast, and ruled over them for over 1,000 years. While it was once a powerful empire, it also had many problems, which caused its eventual collapse.

2   Like many other ancient empires, what is called the Roman Empire can actually be divided into two phases, or stages. These phases are the *republic* and the *empire*. Rome first became powerful as a republic which ruled from about 509 B.C.E. to 45 B.C.E. Being a republic meant that Rome's officials were elected rather than being kings who were born into power. The Roman Republic had a constitution, written laws, and branches of government. If this sounds familiar, it should, because these ideas are the same ones that form the government of the United States! Then, around 45 B.C.E., Julius Caesar seized power and made himself the emperor. This was the start of the phase of the empire. In the empire, the government still functioned, or worked, in almost the same way it had before. The main difference was that the emperor had supreme power over everything. The Roman Empire increased in size by constantly conquering new lands.

3   The Roman Empire reached the height of its power around 117 C.E., but by about 200 C.E., the problems Rome was experiencing led to a decline. The politicians were becoming too corrupt, and civil wars started breaking out between different groups in the empire. Eventually, the empire was so large that it became too difficult to govern from the city of Rome. The Romans came up with

the **solution** of dividing the empire into two empires so that it was easier to manage such a large territory. These were the Western Roman Empire, which was ruled from the city of Rome, and the Eastern Roman Empire, which was ruled from Constantinople, or what we now know as Istanbul in Turkey. However, problems continued in the western part of the empire. The Roman army, once a powerful force, was no longer as strong as it had once been. The problem was that it required a large army to keep control over such a large territory. Romans themselves did not want to serve in the army and began to hire outsiders to serve and fight for them. The population of Rome began to shrink, trade with other nations decreased, and taxes and prices on goods within the Empire increased. The fall of the Roman Empire is usually a reference to the fall of the Western Roman Empire. Around 476 C.E., **barbarians** finally took control of Rome, and many historians consider this the end of the Roman Empire. The fall of Rome had far reaching effects on the lands it had **previously** governed. Rome had provided a strong government, culture, and education for its citizens. With these things gone, much of the area of Europe fell into what is called the *Dark Ages*. Luckily, though, many aspects of the Roman culture were not lost forever.

Activity 1

Revise the following paragraph so that it's more interesting for readers. Combine choppy sentences, reduce run-on sentences, and add structures such as introductory elements so that the passage contains a variety of sentence types. Rewrite your new sentences on the lines provided.

The culture of the Roman Empire has a great influence on our lives today even though we don't think about it much. Romans invented socks (called *soccus*) and shoes as we know them, and some even say they invented cosmetics such as lipstick, and they also invented some ornate jewelry. Romans also used rings. They used them for showing friendship and engagements. They also used the rings at weddings.

_____

_____

_____

_____

_____

_____

Activity 2

1. What does the word **solution** mean? Use clues from the passage to help you determine the meaning.

   _____

   _____

2. What does the word **previously** mean? Use clues from the passage to help you determine the meaning.

   _____

   _____

3. "Collapse of the Roman Empire" includes the word **barbarians**. What does this term mean and how is it related to ancient empires? Use reference materials such as an encyclopedia, dictionary, or the Internet to find out.

   _____

   _____

UNDERSTAND

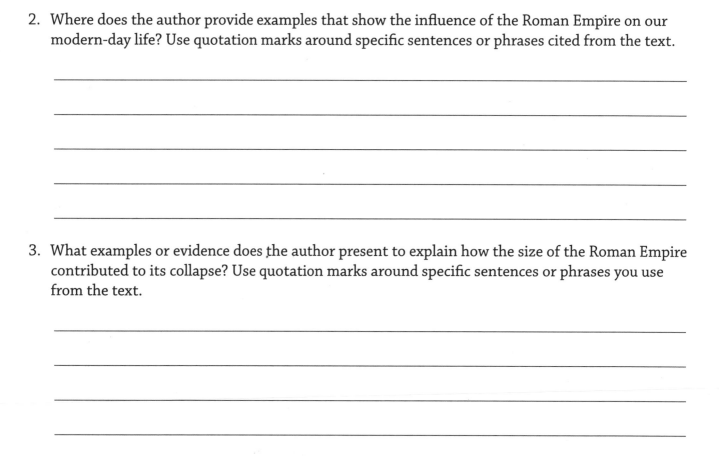

Let's apply the reading skills you covered in this section.

Activity 1

Use "Collapse of the Roman Empire" to answer the following questions.

1. Circle the letter of the sentence that contains a fact-based **summary** of the text.

   A. Several factors, such as size of the empire and civil wars, caused the collapse of the Roman Empire.

   B. The Eastern Roman Empire did not collapse because it was governed better than the other half.

   C. Rome and Constantinople were the capital cities of the Western and Eastern Roman Empire.

   D. The fall of the Roman Empire is usually a reference to the fall of the Western Roman Empire.

2. Where does the author provide examples that show the influence of the Roman Empire on our modern-day life? Use quotation marks around specific sentences or phrases cited from the text.

   _____

   _____

   _____

   _____

   _____

3. What examples or evidence does the author present to explain how the size of the Roman Empire contributed to its collapse? Use quotation marks around specific sentences or phrases you use from the text.

   _____

   _____

   _____

   _____

Standards RI.6.1, RI.6.2, RI.6.3

what's your STORY · DISCOVER

What would you say? Let's take what you have learned and write about it!

Write Your Explanation

Major empires have come and gone in the history of our world, and historians and archaeologists have studied the reasons for the rise and fall of many of these great civilizations. They also have noticed that there tends to be many similarities as well as some differences in the empires themselves. Now it's your turn to become a famous historian! Imagine that you are writing an article for a history textbook that explains the similarities and differences between the cultures of the Egyptian and Roman Empires.

Gathering Information

Step 1: Reread the articles "Decline of the Egyptian Empire" and "Collapse of the Roman Empire."

Step 2: Ask an adult to help you search on the Internet for more information on the Egyptian and Roman Empires. *Hint:* A good search engine to use is *www.google.com*, and you might use the phrases "culture of the Egyptian Empire" or "achievements of the Roman Empire" in your initial search.

Step 3: Read the articles you located and take some notes on the information you discover. *Hint:* When looking for the most important information about an ancient civilization, remember G.R.A.P.E.S.—**G**eography, **R**eligion, **A**ccomplishments, **P**olitics, **E**conomy, **S**ocial structures.

Step 4: Fill out the following Venn diagram, noting both the similarities and the differences between these two once-mighty empires.

Egyptian Empire   Same   Roman Empire

Starting to Write

Step 5: Use the graphic organizer to arrange the information you found in your research and listed on your Venn diagram. Remember to include transition words and to use domain-specific vocabulary.

Topic: Write one or two sentences about your central idea.

_____

_____

Main Idea 1:

_____

_____

Main Idea 2:

_____

_____

Main Idea 3:

_____

_____

Supporting Details:

1. _____

_____

2. _____

_____

3. _____

_____

Supporting Details:

1. _____

_____

2. _____

_____

3. _____

_____

Supporting Details:

1. _____

_____

2. _____

_____

3. _____

_____

Conclusion: Write one or two sentences to summarize your central idea and conclude the essay in a meaningful way.

_____

_____

Step 6: Take the information from your graphic organizer and write out your explanation (main points and supporting details) in complete sentences. Be sure to include transition words and phrases to link your ideas!

Transition Words and Phrases You Might Choose To Use

for instance	also	in fact	for example	first	although
for this reason	in addition	however	therefore	finally	next

*Remember to use a comma after transition words that begin sentences!

Step 7: Ask an adult to read what you have written. Work together to do the following:

- Make sure you have presented three topics or areas in which there are similarities or differences between the two cultures.

- Proofread to make sure your tone is more formal because you are writing for a textbook audience.

- Remove all instances of "I" and "you" from your essay.

- Revise in places where you can make better word choices. Choose a few words from your essay and consult a thesaurus to see if you can choose better words to use.

- Edit your paper for errors in grammar and mechanics.

- Pay special attention to commas with introductory elements and items in a series.

Biomes of the World

We have a responsibility to care for the environment and to make sure that it is healthy enough to support future generations of people as well as the wide range of plant and animal species that live in it. Biomes are large areas of the world with similar climates (weather patterns), plant life, and animal life. They are grouped as terrestrial (land) biomes, such as a tundra or a desert, and aquatic (water) biomes, such as a coral reef, or a wetland. As the human population increases and technology advances, the world's biomes have been negatively affected. People drive cars, cut down trees, and clear forest lands to raise cattle and build cities, all of which contribute to global warming and change the climates around the world. When we educate ourselves about these issues, we can begin to take steps to reverse some of the damage. This unit brings awareness to some of these issues and discusses ways to address them.

Note: The references to authors, articles, and websites are purely fictitious in this workbook. These have been added to help students recognize, classify, and understand the different types of source material and how to assess if it is credible or not, as some of the Common Core Standards require.

Siberian Tundra
Melting Permafrost Threatens Thriving Siberian Habitats

By Kelly Michaels, *The Environmental Journal*, August 2014

1 On a cold, windy day in the tundra, researchers march through several feet of snow and ice to get to their study site. They have been working for months at this point to figure out the rate at which the frozen layer is melting.

2 The tundra, which refers to areas where a layer of permanently frozen deep soil exists, covers about twenty percent of the Earth's surface and stretches across the northern hemisphere in Asia, North America, and Europe. It has two layers of soil: the active layer and the **permafrost**. While the active layer freezes and melts with the seasons, the permafrost layer stays frozen. Winters are long, windy, and cold; summers are cool and short.

3 The Siberian tundra is located in northeastern Russia. During winter, temperatures sometimes reach –40 degrees Fahrenheit (–40 degrees Celsius), and the ground is covered with snow and ice. The permafrost layer in the Siberian tundra can be as deep as 1,968 feet. Winds travel between thirty and sixty miles per hour and can freeze bare skin in about thirty seconds. Summers in the tundra are like the fall and winter seasons in the United States, with temperatures only reaching between 37 to 54 degrees Fahrenheit (3 to 12 degrees Celsius). When the ice and snow melt, they consequently form puddles called **thermokarsts**; therefore, the summers in the tundra are also marshy. This means that the ground is a muddy soup! Furthermore, three rivers, the Lena, Ob, and Yenisei, flow into the Siberian tundra and form **pingoes**. Pingoes are up to three hundred-feet tall and half mile-wide

Reindeer in front of pools.

glossary

Infrastructure: The basic equipment and structures (such as roads and bridges) that are needed for a country, region, or organization to function properly.

Permafrost: A layer of soil that is always frozen in very cold regions of the world.

Pingoes: Very large pools of water that freeze underground and push the ground up to form hills.

Thermokarsts: Puddles that are a result of ice and snow melt in the tundra.

pools of water that freeze underground and push the ground up to form hills. Because there is only about six to ten inches of snowfall, the tundra is like a desert.

4   Although the Siberian tundra has harsh weather conditions, some plant and animal life thrive here. Plants include fungus, grass, and shrubs, which grow low to the ground and group together to stay warm. They also have tiny hairs on their leaves to help keep in moisture. Animals include fish, mammals, insects, and birds, which typically stay only for the summer. In order to adapt, these animals have thick fur and extra layers of fat to help them stay warm. Like the plants, animals are low to the ground because this prevents them from losing heat.

5   For a long time, researchers have suspected that the tundra is the center of global warming. Yet, scientists have remained in the dark about the release of greenhouse gases from melting permafrost. Recent studies of Siberian caves, however, suggest that the permafrost layer over a significant part of Siberia could melt if global temperatures increase by 1.5 degrees Celsius. If this were to happen, more than one trillion tons of greenhouse gases like carbon dioxide and methane would be released into the atmosphere. Russian scientist Sergey Zimov explains that in the Siberian tundra, "total carbon storage is similar to that of all the rain forests of our planets put together." In these studies, researchers observed stalagmites and stalactites, mineral formations which only grow when rainwater and snow drip into caves. Because the stalagmites and stalactites represent 500,000 years of changing permafrost conditions, scientists are able to estimate how warmer climates affect the tundra. An increase in global temperatures could be harmful to plant and animal life in the Siberian tundra, as well as to the human environment. Scientists in the area, for instance, note that roads, railways, power lines, and businesses are all built on permafrost; the melting of the permafrost could damage the **infrastructure** of the communities in the Siberian tundra.

6   Most researchers agree that daily human activities such as driving or producing electricity also create extra amounts of carbon dioxide, methane, and other greenhouse gases in the atmosphere, trapping heat and creating a warming effect. The effect is even greater in polar regions like the tundra. For example, the Arctic is responsible for about nine percent of the methane that is released into the atmosphere. When Katey Walter Anthony, researcher at the University of Alaska Fairbanks, studied Arctic lakes in Alaska, Canada, and Russia, she found that methane was leaking from holes at the bottom of the lakes. When interviewed, she said "The permafrost gets digested in the guts of the lake and burped out as methane." At the time, she also noted that more than fifty billion tons of methane could be released from Siberian lakes alone.

7   Further evidence suggests that the permafrost layer has already begun to release methane gas into the atmosphere. Recently, scientists located a crater at the Yamal Peninsula in Siberia and now believe that the crater was created by the release of methane gas from the melting layer. According to researchers, air near the bottom of the crater contained about 9.6 percent methane. In contrast, the air we breathe normally contains about 0.000179 percent methane. They believe that as a result of a 5 degree Celsius increase in temperatures during the 2012 and 2013 summer seasons, permafrost melted and released the methane that had been trapped inside. The "gas pressure increased until the ground popped like a balloon," explained a German researcher, Hans-Wolfgang Hubberten.

8   Researchers worry that recent findings, along with the discovery of two new craters in Siberia, indicate that there will be changes to the Siberian climate as well as its local habitats and environments. This could mean fallen buildings, eroded soil (worn away), destroyed ecosystems, and distressed communities.

DETERMINING POINT OF VIEW AND PURPOSE

Point of View: This is an author's expressed opinion or view on a topic within a text.

Purpose: The reason why a text was written. The three purposes are as follows:
- To inform (or teach) • To persuade (or convince) • To entertain

Use "Siberian Tundra" to answer the following questions.

1. Which statement best reflects the **author's purpose** for writing the article?
    A. Even though the Siberian tundra is cold and windy, there are lots of plant and animal life.
    B. The Siberian Tundra makes up about 20% of the Earth's surface and spans three continents.
    C. Recently, scientists discovered craters in the Siberian tundra in areas where permafrost had melted.
    D. The Siberian Tundra is in trouble because of global warming caused by the release of greenhouse gases into the atmosphere.

2. Which of the following statements best explains the author's **point of view**?
    A. Craters are destroying the living environments in the Siberian tundra.
    B. Researchers need to do more to figure out why the permafrost is melting.
    C. The melting permafrost could potentially destroy the Siberian tundra habitat and ecosystem.
    D. The Siberian tundra only has a few plant and animal species, so it's not a big deal if habitats are destroyed.

3. Does the author clearly express her point of view? Explain your answer.

    _____

    _____

    _____

    _____

EXPAND YOUR KNOWLEDGE:
The summer season in the tundra is only about fifty to sixty days. During this time, the sun shines for twenty-four hours a day, and some plants grow. To read more about the tundra, go to this link: *http://environment.nationalgeographic.com/ environment/habitats/tundra-profile/*

UNDERSTANDING FIGURATIVE LANGUAGE

Figurative Language: Sets of words or phrases that stand for more than their literal, or actual, meaning. Examples of figurative language include similes and metaphors.

Simile: Compares two unlike things using the words *like* or *as*.

> Example: Melody cleared her plate **like** a vacuum cleaner swallows dust.

Metaphor: Compares two unlike things, but does not use the words *like* or *as*.

> Example: The snow was a white carpet.

Connotative Language: Ideas or feelings associated with a word, but are not part of that word's meaning. A word's connotation can be positive (good), negative (bad), or neutral (in the middle; not one way or the other).

> Example: The word **dove** has positive connotations because it is often associated with peace.

Activity 1

Use "Siberian Tundra" to think about the word choices the author made and whether they are figurative or connotative language. Answer the following questions.

1. Which of the following sentences from the article is an example of a **simile**?
   A. *"Summers in the tundra are like the fall and winter seasons in the United States."*
   B. *"The permafrost layer in the Siberian tundra can be as deep as 1,968 feet."*
   C. *"The gas pressure increased until the ground popped like a balloon."*
   D. *"The effect is even greater in polar regions like the tundra."*

2. Reread the third paragraph of the article. What **metaphor** is used in the paragraph, and what two things does it compare?

   _____

   _____

   _____

Activity 2

Indicate whether each of the following words has a positive, negative, or neutral connotation.

1. global warming _____

2. ecosystem _____

3. communities _____

4. summer _____

5. stalagmites and stalactites _____

Stalagmites and stalactites in a cave.

USING PRONOUNS CORRECTLY

Pronouns are words that take the place of nouns in a sentence. Pronouns can be singular and reflect the first person (I, me, mine), second person (you, your, yours), or third person (it, him, she, his, hers). They can also be plural and reflect the first person (we, us, our, ours), second person (you, your, yours), or third person (they, them, their, theirs). In order to understand what they are reading, students must pay attention to pronoun shifts, and vague, case, and intensive pronouns.

Pronoun Shift: A grammatical error in which the author starts a sentence using one type of pronoun and suddenly switches to another; this can confuse the reader.

> **Example:** **Incorrect:** If you eat a balanced diet, most people can maintain their weight.
> **Correct:** If **you** eat a balanced diet, **you** can maintain your weight.

Vague Pronouns: When writers use pronouns to refer to a prior idea, but the reference is unclear.

> **Example:** **Incorrect:** Lucas dislikes Murphy, but he is friendly. (Who is the friendly one?)
> **Correct:** Lucas dislikes Murphy, even though Murphy is friendly.

Digging Deeper

The melting permafrost and subsequent release of methane gas into the atmosphere has a wide range of consequences, including sinking holes in the ground that cause buildings and communities to collapse. To watch a video about the impact of warming temperatures on different environments, visit this website: www.nbclearn.com/changingplanet/cuecard/52627

Activity 1

1. Read the following sentences from the article and indicate whether they reflect a pronoun shift or vague pronoun.

   "Researchers worry that recent findings, along with the discovery of two new craters in Siberia, indicate that there will be changes to the Siberian climate as well as its local habitats and environments. This could mean fallen buildings, eroded soil (worn away), destroyed ecosystems, and distressed communities."

   This is an example of _____

2. Fix the sentences from the previous question so that the ideas expressed are clearer.

   _____

   _____

   _____

   _____

   _____

Vague pronouns can be fixed by adding the word **which** into the sentence and placing a noun that makes sense before it in the sentence.

> Example: **Incorrect:** I stopped eating jawbreakers. This rots my teeth.
> **Correct:** I stopped eating jawbreakers, a candy **which** rots my teeth.

3. Fix the following sentence.

   "When the ice and snow melt, they consequently form puddles called thermokarsts; therefore, the summers in the tundra are also marshy. This means that the ground is a muddy soup!"

   _____

   _____

   _____

Activity 2

Case Pronouns: There are three types of cases in which an author can use pronouns: the subjective case, the objective case, and the possessive case.

Subjective Case: Pronouns used as subjects
(I, you, he, we, it, who, they).

Objective Case: Pronouns used as objects of verbs or prepositions
(me, you, them, him, us, her, whom).

Possessive Case: Pronouns used to express ownership
(mine, yours, hers, is, ours, whose, theirs).

Intensive Pronouns: Pronouns used to intensify or strengthen a statement
(myself, themselves, ourselves).

1. Match the following sentences from the article with the correct case pronoun. Write the number that corresponds to the type of pronoun case in the box next to the sentence.

Sentence from the Article		Type of Pronoun Case
A. They have been working for months at this point to figure out the rate at which the frozen layer is melting.		1. Possessive Case
B. Like the plants, animals are low to the ground because this prevents them from losing heat.		2. Subjective Case
C. They also have tiny hairs on their leaves to help keep in moisture.		3. Objective Case

2. Rewrite the following sentence using an intensive pronoun.

    Most researchers agree that daily human activities such as driving or producing electricity also create extra amounts of carbon dioxide, methane, and other greenhouse gases in the atmosphere, trapping heat and creating a warming effect.

    _____

    _____

    _____

    _____

UNDERSTANDING VOCABULARY

After reading "Siberian Tundra," use context clues, word relationships, or a dictionary to help you answer the following questions.

1. What is the meaning of **infrastructure** in the following sentence?

   "Scientists in the area, for instance, note that roads, railways, power lines, and businesses are all built on permafrost; the melting of the permafrost could damage the **infrastructure** *of the communities in the Siberian tundra."*

   A. layers
   B. systems
   C. civilizations
   D. physical organization

Sunset on the tundra.

2. What does the author mean by the phrase **"remained in the dark"** in the following sentence?

   "Yet, scientists have **remained in the dark** *about the release of greenhouse gases from melting permafrost."*

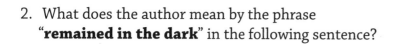

CAUSE AND EFFECT RELATIONSHIPS

Cause: An action that makes something else happen.

Effect: The result of that action.

Cause and effect relationships are **signaled** by words and phrases such as *because, so, since, as, consequently, therefore, as a result of, due to, yet, in order to, accordingly, if, then, for this reason, nevertheless, because of,* and *this led to*.

Example: In order to adapt, these animals have thick fur and extra layers of fat to help them stay warm.

Sentences can be rewritten to show cause and effect relationships.

> **Example:** Cassie went to the store after 9 p.m., and the store was closed.
> **Rewritten:** The store was closed **because** Cassie arrived after 9 p.m.

Adding **because** shows a cause and effect relationship.

Read this sentence from "Siberian Tundra."

*"**When** the ice and snow melt, they **consequently** form puddles called thermokarsts."*

Think about the two bolded words **when** and **consequently**.

1. What kind of relationship do these words show?

   _____

   _____

2. How do they help the reader to better understand the information in the text?

   _____

   _____

Challenge: Rewrite the following sentences to include words that show a cause and effect relationship.

1. Winds travel between 30 and 60 miles per hour and can freeze bare skin in about thirty seconds.

   _____

   _____

2. Scientists in the area, for instance, note that roads, railways, power lines, and businesses are all built on permafrost; the melting of the permafrost could damage the infrastructure of the communities in the Siberian tundra.

   _____

   _____

   _____

   _____

| Home | About Me | The Wonder of the Amazon | Resources |

The Wonder of the Amazon

By Luca Noel
The Wonder of the Amazon copied from
http://lucasscienceclass.net

Jaguar.

1   Welcome to my site! I have been following the Amazon Rainforest since fourth grade when I had to do a project on global habitats. Since then, the Amazon has experienced droughts, has decreased in size, and has been affected by climate change. I started this blog as a way to keep track of all the changing weather patterns around the world and show how the Amazon fits into the larger picture.

2   Rainforests are usually described as hot, humid, and wet. They have the widest range of plants and animals on Earth! The Amazon is an example of a rainforest. Located in South America, the Amazon takes up about forty percent of Brazil's geographical area. Parts of the rainforest are also in eight other countries: Bolivia, Peru, Ecuador, Colombia, Venezuela, Guyana, Suriname, and French Guiana. It's been said that the Amazon has about 1.4 billion acres of thick, dense forests, and ten percent of the world's known species live there! The rainforest is home to some jaguars, pink dolphins, birds, butterflies, two-toed sloths, and various species of monkeys, to name a few. Additionally, over 40,000 plant and 3,000 freshwater fish species, along with over 370 types of reptiles can be found there. Even though the forests are filled with giant trees and some wild animals, more than thirty million people, including 350 indigenous groups (people who are native to the land), also live there.

TABLE 1: Rainfall Levels in Manaus, Brazil

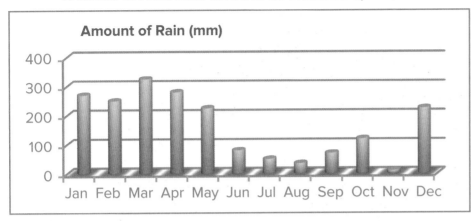

These people depend on the forest for food, shelter, clothing, and traditional medicines.

3   In Manaus, Brazil, which is considered to be the **Heart of the Amazon**, the rainy season is from December to May. The amount of rainfall is calculated in millimeters, often written as mm. Because there are high amounts of water vapor in the air, the Amazon is said to have high humidity. Table 1 shows the differences in rainfall levels in Manaus from January to December.

4   Rainfall and high humidity contribute to the growth of different types of vegetation, groups of plants, bushes, grasses, and trees. There are four types of vegetation that grow in rainforests; the shrub layer, the under canopy, the canopy, and the emergents. The shrub layer is at the bottom of the rainforest and gets very dark. This layer can even flood during times of heavy rainfall. While the under canopy sits a little higher than the shrub layer, only baby trees, known as saplings, grow here. They wait for larger plants and trees to die, and then grow in those spaces. The canopy is the third level from the ground and is usually about sixty-five to 130 feet tall. Different types of bugs, birds, and small mammals live in the canopy. At the very top are the emergents; they are much higher so they get a lot of sunlight. Table 2 shows how much sunlight three of the four types of rainforest vegetation receive.

TABLE 2: Rate of Sunlight Received by Vegetation

	High	Medium	Low
Canopy		X	
Emergents	X		
Shrubs			X

San Rafael Falls, Ecuador.

| Home | About Me | The Wonder of the Amazon | Resources |

Flowering Amazon plant.

5   Research suggests that there is a connection between how well the Amazon is doing and whether or not planet Earth is healthy. If the Amazon stops thriving, it could harm the Earth! The Amazon contains billions of tons of carbon, which helps to make the climate more stable. If people continue to cut down the trees and clear the land for other uses, a process called deforestation, the carbon will be released into the air and contribute to global warming. Deforestation currently contributes to about 340 million tons of carbon released into the air annually.

6   At this point, you might be wondering why people would chop down the trees in the Amazon and clear the land for other purposes! As the demand for products like beef and soy increases, farmers cut down trees to create more space to grow crops and to graze cattle. Also, as big farming companies clear land in the forests, they push out smaller farmers, who are then forced to clear more land in order to make money and feed themselves and their families. Currently, eighty percent of the land that has been cleared in the Amazon is used to raise cattle. Unfortunately, some of the products farmers use on the land also pollute the rivers, or make them impure. Furthermore, some farmers may use fires to clear the land; the fires can quickly spread and destroy more forestland than intended.

7   As the local governments in the areas surrounding the Amazon have built roads and developed policies to help organize their cities, they have also disturbed life in the Amazon. For example, the

building of dams to meet the needs of energy demands in Brazil has prevented many species from reaching their water sources. Dams have also destroyed some of the 4,100 miles of rivers in the Amazon! Each year, the Amazon loses forestland the size of the state of Delaware.

8   To address some of these problems, organizations such as the World Wildlife Foundation (WWF) are working with local governments to secure the land. In Brazil, for example, the foundation created the Amazon Region Protected Areas Program (ARPA) to protect some parks covering about 150 million acres of land. The size of this area is almost twice as large as all of the national parks in the United States combined! ARPA also helps the wildlife in the area adapt to the warmer temperatures and makes sure that local farmers can protect their crops from drought and high levels of rainfall. In 2002, ARPA worked with the Brazilian government to create Tumucumaque Mountains National Park, which is the largest protected tropical forest in the world. The park has nine and a half million acres of land and protects various animals, including jaguars, anteaters, harpy eagles, and the black-beard saki, a rare monkey breed. The World Wildlife Foundation is always looking for new and exciting ways to educate people about the Amazon and how important it is to protect its lands, trees, rivers, species, and people.

Amazon milk frog.

UNDERSTANDING FIGURATIVE LANGUAGE

Authors of informational texts make choices about which words and phrases to use in order to best convey, or express, their ideas to their readers. They may use figurative language to convey their ideas.

Figurative Language: Sets of words or phrases that stand for more than their literal, or actual, meaning. Examples of figurative language include similes and metaphors.

Simile: Compares two unlike things using the words *like* or *as*.

> Example: Melody cleared her plate like a vacuum cleaner swallows dust.

Metaphor: Compares two unlike things, but does not use the words *like* or *as*.

> Example: The snow was a thick blanket of white covering the mountain.

Use "The Wonder of the Amazon" to answer the following questions.

1. Read the following sentence from the passage:

    *"In Manaus, Brazil, which is considered to be the **Heart of the Amazon**, the rainy season is from December to May."*

    Is **Heart of the Amazon** a simile or a metaphor? Explain your answer.

    _____

    _____

    _____

    _____

2. What does **Heart of the Amazon** mean?

    _____

    _____

    _____

    _____

Trail through Amazon.

COMBINING IDEAS

You can combine ideas from different sources in order to get a better understanding of a topic.

Information can be presented in a variety of **media**, or in different **formats** and styles. Using information from different sources can help a reader develop a better understanding of a topic, idea, or issue.

Media: Tools that allow people to communicate their ideas, including radio, television, newspapers, magazines, books, and the Internet, to name a few. Media is the plural form of medium.

Format: The way in which something is arranged or organized.

Use the information in the text and tables in "The Wonder of the Amazon" to answer the following questions.

1. When is the rainy season in the Amazon? In which month during the rainy season does it rain the most? In which month during the rainy season does it rain the least?

   _____

   _____

   _____

2. Look at Table 2 in "The Wonder of the Amazon." The table only shows three of the four types of vegetation described in the text. "Under Canopy" is missing. Based on the information presented in the text and in the table, place an X in the circle that shows how much sunlight the "under canopy" receives.

TABLE 2: Rate of Sunlight Received by Vegetation

Amount of Sunlight	Canopy	Emergents	Shrubs	Under Canopy
High		X		◯
Between High and Medium				◯
Medium	X			◯
Between Medium and Low				◯
Low			X	◯

3. How much sunlight does the under canopy receive compared to other types of vegetation?_____

USING PUNCTUATION CORRECTLY

Parentheses are used to include information that may not be important, but the author wants to include anyway. The information inside the parentheses may be interesting, but would not change the meaning of the sentence if it were missing. This is what parentheses looks like: ( ); the information appears inside of the two marks. The parentheses must be used to set off nonrestrictive/parenthetical elements.

A **nonrestrictive element** is a word, phrase, or dependent clause that provides added (unimportant) information to a sentence. It is usually set off with commas or dashes. A **parenthetical element** is any sentence element that interrupts the forward movement of the clause.

> **Example:** The statue of the famous artist from 1896 has recently gathered much attention for its unique design.
>
> **This can be changed to:**
> The statue of the famous artist (from 1896) has recently gathered much attention for its unique design.

Standards RI.6.7, L.6.2.a

Rewrite the following sentences using parentheses to set off nonrestrictive elements.

1. Rainfall and high humidity contribute to the growth of the different types of vegetation, groups of plants, bushes, grass, and trees.

_____

_____

_____

_____

2. If people continue to cut down the trees and clear the land for other uses, a process called deforestation, the carbon will be released into the air and contribute to global warming.

_____

_____

_____

_____

_____

3. The WWF organization represented in 100 countries is connecting with local governments in Brazil to secure land in the Amazon to prevent deforestation.

_____

_____

_____

_____

EXPAND YOUR KNOWLEDGE:
To learn more about Brazil, where the majority of the Amazon Rainforest is located, visit the following website:
http://kids.nationalgeographic.com/explore/countries/ brazil/

CONDUCTING RESEARCH

There are instances when you, the reader, will still have questions about topics discussed in the text. If the answers aren't in the text, it may require just a little research to find the answers that you need.

Use "The Wonder of the Amazon" to complete this activity.

In the text, the author states that Brazil's increasing demand for energy has led to the building of dams that have negatively affected the species in the Amazon. Research this topic and find out exactly how the dams prevent the different species from reaching their water source. Use the space provided to write down your notes and ideas from your research.

Source 1: _____

_____   _____

_____   _____

_____   _____

_____   _____

Source 2: _____

_____   _____

_____   _____

_____   _____

_____   _____

Source 3: _____

_____   _____

_____   _____

_____   _____

_____   _____

After you complete your research, explain what you learned about the effect of dams on the Amazon rainforest in the space provided.

_____

_____

_____

_____

_____

_____

_____

_____

CREDIBLE SOURCES

It is important to know the following when researching sources:

Information may come from a credible or non-credible source. A **credible** source is trustworthy because the claims in the text are supported by proper evidence. Writers should always use credible sources. A **non-credible** source is the opposite of a credible source.

Credible sources include encyclopedias, well-known newspapers like the _New York Times_, published journals, non-fiction books, and some websites, especially those connected to the government, to schools, or professional groups.

Non-credible sources include various social media, research articles that have claims that are not supported by evidence, blogs, personal websites, fictional books and films, and websites that try to persuade people to believe something that may not be true or that are selling things to people.

1. Of the two sources listed in this unit, "Siberian Tundra" and "The Wonder of the Amazon," which is **most credible**? Why?

_____

_____

_____

_____

_____

UNIT 5

Nature's Effect on the World

You can be fascinated by the beauty and sheer power of Earth's natural elements that create a variety of weather patterns, yet at the same time, you may not always understand them. In this unit, you will discover how nature has changed the face of the Earth over time—natural disasters have wiped out civilizations, disrupted communities, and forever changed the landscape of various parts of the world. This unit gives you the opportunity to learn about some of these disasters and to reflect on just how powerful nature can be in shaping the world and the people living in it.

Note: The references to authors, articles, and websites are purely fictitious in this workbook. These have been added to help students recognize, classify, and understand the different types of source material and how to assess if it is credible or not, as some of the Common Core Standards require.

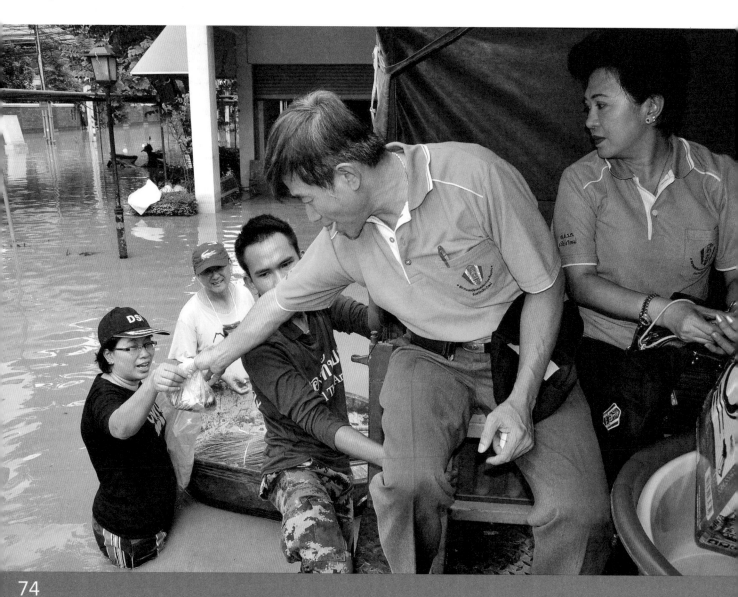

The Lost City of Pompeii

1   Ahh! Life was good in Pompeii. Tens of thousands of people loved gathering in its open squares and marketplaces to enjoy all that the town had to offer. The area attracted rich families and people on vacation, especially those who lived luxurious lives and wanted a change in scenery. Located about five miles from Mount Vesuvius, Pompeii was a beautiful town with elegant villas (upper-class country homes) and paved streets. Its streets were lined with fine artisan (craft) shops, cafes, small factories, and bathhouses.

2   However, on one fateful day in 79 C.E., Mount Vesuvius, a volcano that had remained somewhat inactive in previous years, **erupted** and destroyed the bustling, beautiful town of Pompeii. Located by the Bay of Naples in Italy, Mount Vesuvius is hundreds of thousands of years old, and according to historians, the volcano had erupted about fifty times before over the course of the years. When the volcano erupted a 100-mile-per-hour gush of overly heated poisonous gas and rock shot down Mount Vesuvius, engulfing, or swallowing up, everything in its path. As thick volcanic dust and smoke filled the air, it became impossible for people to move and breathe. As a result, thousands of people died and Pompeii was buried beneath hot lava and ashes, never to be seen for thousands of years! Some eye witnesses of the event said that "the dust poured across the land like a flood" and covered the city in darkness. A young writer by the name of Pliny watched from across the bay as Mount Vesuvius erupted. In his works, he described the volcano's eruption as a "cloud of unusual size and appearance," and compared it to a pine tree that "rose to a great height on a sort of trunk and then split off into branches." Today, geologists refer to volcanic eruptions the size of Mount Vesuvius' as "Plinean eruptions."

Tourists visit Pompeii—an ancient Roman city that was ruined from the eruption of Mount Vesuvius in 79 A.D.

Wall art from Herculaneum, a town near Pompeii.

3   No longer a thriving metropolis, Pompeii became a ruined site with much history to tell. In 1748, explorers discovered the city of Pompeii under a carpet of volcanic ash. To their surprise, the site remained intact; the volcanic ash had protected the site, serving as a kind of **preservative**. Explorers were able to **excavate** old buildings, art, and skeletons, all of which teach us about the ancient world of Pompeii and how it once stood.

4   **Volcanologists** have been working for years to figure out what caused Mount Vesuvius to erupt without warning on that fateful day. Researchers say that the violent volcano did not form in one day. Instead, it was like an angry animal with a temper, waiting to explode. Looking back, scientists note that before the volcano's eruption in 79 C.E., a huge earthquake hit the region in an area known as Campania in 63 C.E. Because the quake happened sixteen years earlier, perhaps no one thought to see it for what it was—a warning that Mount Vesuvius would soon erupt!

5   Although Mount Vesuvius has not erupted since 1944, experts believe that it will erupt again shortly, as it is one of the most dangerous volcanoes in the world. A Vesuvian eruption today would be another disaster, to say the least, because currently, about three million people live within twenty miles of the volcano's crater. In the meantime, explorers continue to excavate the site of ancient Pompeii. To some, the site is still as fascinating and as mysterious as it was when it was first uncovered in 1748.

Digging Deeper

Make Your Own Volcano!
Demonstrate volcanic activity by making our very own working homemade volcano! Visit the following website:
http://www.crystal-clear-science-fair-projects.com/volcano- science-project.html

CENTRAL IDEAS, KEY DETAILS, AND SUMMARIES

Use "The Lost City of Pompeii" to answer the following questions.

1. Which of the following statements **best** reflects the **central idea** of the text?

    A. Mount Vesuvius is one of the most powerful volcanoes in the world that researchers cannot explain.

    B. Pompeii was a beautiful, luxurious town until Mount Vesuvius erupted hundreds of years ago, changing the city forever.

    C. Researchers need to do a better job of explaining how Mt. Vesuvius erupted and why it harmed so many people.

    D. Mount Vesuvius is one of the most dangerous volcanoes in the world, but it has not erupted since 1944.

2. How does the author introduce and analyze the central idea?

    _____

    _____

    _____

3. Provide a **summary** of the text. Remember to restate the main idea and list the supporting details in your own words. If you use language directly from the text, remember to use quotation marks.

    _____

    _____

    _____

    _____

    _____

EXPAND YOUR KNOWLEDGE:
Nature has an incredible effect on the world and how it changes over time. To learn more about how the volcanic eruption at Mount Vesuvius shaped Pompeii, visit:
http://www.history.com/topics/ancient- history/pompeii

MAKING WORDS

Many words in the English language are formed by taking basic Latin or Greek words and adding combinations of prefixes and suffixes to them.

Prefix: An affix that is placed before the stem of the word or the root word. Common Latin and Greek prefixes and their meanings include: **amphi—both, ab—away, extra—outside, contra—against**

Suffix: An affix that is placed after the stem of the word or the root word. Common suffixes and their meanings include: **ic—like, tion—being, ist—one who**

Root word: A basic word to which a prefix or suffix is added. Common Latin and Greek roots and their meanings include: **ambi—two, aqua—water, dynam—power, terra—earth, act—do**

> **Example:** The word **microscope** actually has two root words, *micro* and *scope*. *Micro* means small and *scope* means viewing instrument.

1. Based on the root words and affixes listed in this lesson, determine the meaning of the following words.

    Dynamic _____

    Amphitheater _____

    Abnormal _____

    Extraterrestrial _____

    Action _____

2. Use each of the words you just defined in question 1 in a sentence.

    _____

    _____

    _____

    _____

    _____

    _____

    _____

UNDERSTANDING VOCABULARY

Use "The Lost City of Pompeii" to answer the following questions.

1. Read the following sentence from the passage.

   *"However, on one fateful day in 79 C.E., Mount Vesuvius, a volcano that had remained somewhat inactive in previous years, **erupted** and destroyed the bustling, beautiful town of Pompeii."*

   What does **erupted** mean?

   _____

2. Read the following sentence from the passage.

   *"**Volcanologists** have been working for years to figure out what caused Mount Vesuvius to erupt without warning."*

   What does a **volcanologist** do?

   A. Digs caves

   B. Studies old cities

   C. Studies volcanoes

   D. Digs volcanoes

Authors may use words you have never heard of in a text. The context of the article you are reading can help you figure out what these words mean. Look at the surrounding words and sentences to help you determine the unknown word's meaning.

3. What does **excavate** mean in the following sentence?

   *"Explorers were able to **excavate** old buildings, art, and skeletons, all of which teach us about the ancient world of Pompeii and how it once stood."*

   A. To dig up

   B. To clean

   C. To cover up

   D. To bury in the ground

4. What does the word **preservative** mean in the following sentence?

   *"To their surprise, the site remained intact; the volcanic ash had protected the site, serving as a kind of **preservative**."*

   _____

Bodies buried under ash in Pompeii.

The Weather Magazine
January 2013

Tsunamis—Waves Without Borders

1   Plan ahead, get prepared, be ready—because when natural disasters strike, there is no time to spare! Entire communities have disappeared at the hands of catastrophic natural events! In 2011, for example, a small fishing port in Japan, called Minamisanriku, disappeared after a tsunami \(t)soo-ˈnä-mē\ struck. Do you know what a tsunami is? A tsunami is a series of ocean waves that are caused as a result of movement in the ocean floor. These movements include volcanic activity, landslides, or even earthquakes. The majority of recorded tsunamis occur in the Pacific and Indian Oceans. While tsunamis can sometimes be harmless and result in waves that are only a few inches tall, they can also cause destruction, devastating everything in their paths, as did the tsunami that hit Minamisanriku, Japan. As a result, history was forever changed.

The March 11 earthquake generated a devastating tsunami that was observed all over the Pacific and caused tremendous devastation locally, including an accident at the Fukushima Daiichi Nuclear Power Plant.

2   The mayor of the town, Jin Sato, recalls that the disaster began at around 2:46 p.m. on March 11. Sato was headed home from a meeting about how to increase the town's tsunami readiness activities when the earthquake struck, and a 280-mile-long section of the Earth's crust moved suddenly. After five minutes of nonstop shaking, the earthquake finally stopped. However, at this point, the ocean began to toss and **hurl** waves so gigantic that they crashed over the town's eighteen-foot-high seawall. As Sato and some of his friends watched the waves from a disaster readiness center, homes and communities collapsed as the ocean swept them away.

3   Researchers report that Japan has the best emergency readiness programs for earthquakes and tsunamis. Local weather people and seismologists (people who study earthquakes) knew a severe earthquake was coming, but they were **optimistic** because they were prepared for it. However, a complication arose due to the tsunami. This was an unexpected effect of the earthquake.

4   Although this Japanese community had advanced tsunami systems in place, the systems did not work effectively. For instance, early on, the system **predicted** that the earthquake was going to have a **magnitude** of 7.9; however, later on, scientists learned that the earthquake was actually a magnitude of 9. This means that the actual earthquake was about twelve times greater than what researchers had predicted. Also, while news reports warned people that tsunami waves would be about ten feet, the waves actually reached fifty feet. Since then, local leaders and scientists have been working together to ensure that nothing like this ever happens again.

5   Tsunamis have hit somewhere in the world almost yearly since the times of Ancient Greece, and even before they could be recorded. The big ones have been significant enough to have changed the course of history. About 3,500 years ago, for example, a tsunami struck the island of Crete. Historians believe that this disaster is what led to the downfall of the Minoans, a complex civilization that lived there. Moreover, in 1755, an earthquake and tsunami struck Lisbon, Portugal, causing massive destruction.

6   The effects of earthquakes and tsunamis are undoubtedly hard to recover from, and are often long-lasting. It is very hard for people to go back to the normal affairs of life. That being the case, small nonprofit organizations and schools have been established to spread awareness about earthquakes and tsunamis and to educate those who live in "danger zones," such as communities close to the ocean. It is important that people are provided with proper information so they can make informed decisions about where to go, what to do, and how to cope with disasters.

The red dot on the map shows the location of the earthquake which caused the March 11 tsunami in Japan.

glossary

Hurl: To throw something with force.

Magnitude: A number that shows the power of an earthquake.

Optimistic: Believing that good things will happen in the future.

Predict: To say that something will or might happen in the future.

CENTRAL IDEAS, KEY DETAILS, AND SUMMARIES

Use "Tsunamis—Waves Without Borders" to answer the following questions.

1. Which of the following statements best reflects the **central idea** of the text?
   A. Tsunamis have destroyed many communities around the world.
   B. Researchers have spent many years searching for causes of tsunamis.
   C. Tsunamis are one example of how nature can shape the environment and change the course of history.
   D. Even though tsunamis have been happening for a long time, scientists are still looking for ways to prepare for and manage them.

2. Cite two pieces of **evidence** from the text that explain how a natural disaster can change the course of history.

   _____

   _____

   _____

   _____

3. What is the central idea in paragraph 3? Provide evidence to support your answer.

   _____

   _____

   _____

4. **Summarize** the text in 3–5 sentences in your own words.

   _____

   _____

   _____

   _____

   _____

SPELLING CORRECTLY

Learning how to spell words not only helps you become a better writer, but it also supports good reading skills. If you are uncertain about how to spell a word, you can always check a dictionary or another reference book, such as a thesaurus.

Each of the following sentences has at least one misspelled word. Write the word(s) correctly on the line provided.

1. A tsunami is absluteley one of the scariest things to live through.

   _____

2. In third grade, I read on the bulettin board at school that an earthquake was coming.

   _____

3. I wonder how scientists distengiush between earthquakes and tsunamis!

   _____

4. I used to think that tails of tsunamis were fabils!

   _____

MAINTAINING STYLE AND PROPER TONE

Style: The type of language used to tell a story.

Tone: The attitude that the story creates.

One way in which authors use consistent style and tone is by using the same verb tense throughout the text.

Example: **INCORRECT:** The doctor explained the patient's symptoms before he asked what **is** wrong.

CORRECT: The doctor explained the patient's symptoms before he asked what **was** wrong.

The following sentences shift verb tense. Circle the wrong verb tense and rewrite the sentence correctly on the lines provided.

1. The mayor of the town remembered that the disaster begun at around 2:46 p.m. that day.

   _____

   _____

2. Seismologists warned people that the tsunami waves are about ten feet, but the waves actually reached fifty feet.

   _____

   _____

3. The government prepared a website and share information about emergency readiness.

   _____

UNDERSTANDING VOCABULARY

Read the following sentences from "Tsunami—Waves Without Borders." Use context clues to determine the meaning of the bold words, and then use a dictionary or other reference book, such as a thesaurus, to make sure that the meaning you wrote is correct.

1. *"For instance, early on, the system predicted that the earthquake was going to have a **magnitude** of 7.9; however, later on, scientists learned that the earthquake was actually a **magnitude** of 9."*

   Your meaning of **magnitude**:

   _____

   Dictionary definition:

   _____

2. *"Local weather people and seismologists (people who study earthquakes) knew a severe earthquake was coming, but they were **optimistic** because they were prepared for it."*

   Your meaning of **optimistic**:

   _____

   Dictionary definition:

   _____

3. *"For instance, early on, the system* **predicted** *that the earthquake* <u>was going to have</u> *a magnitude of 7.9; however, later on, scientists learned that the earthquake was actually a magnitude of 9."*

Your meaning of **predicted**:

_____

Dictionary definition:

_____

4. *"However, at this point, the ocean began to toss and* **hurl** *waves so gigantic that they crashed over the town's eighteen-foot-high seawall."*

Your meaning of **hurl**:

_____

Dictionary definition:

_____

USING EVIDENCE AND SOURCES

Types of Evidence

First-hand information: Research based on interviews, experiments, research studies, personal experiences.

Second-hand information: Research based on various texts prepared by other authors such as books, magazines, and websites.

Credible vs. Non-Credible Sources

Credible: Sources you can trust because the author backs up his or her claims and ideas with evidence.

> **Examples:** Books by well-respected experts in their field, government or educational university websites

Non-Credible: Sources that cannot be trusted because there is no solid evidence presented to back up the claims.

> **Examples:** Social media, self-authored websites, websites trying to persuade you to do something, articles over ten years old, research articles without citations (references to other authors' works where information was obtained)

1. You are preparing a research report for class about different types of natural disasters. Which of the following sources would you most likely use?

   A. A blog

   B. A news article

   C. A cartoon based upon real events

   D. A film uploaded to a shared website

2. Explain your answer for question 1.

   _____

   _____

3. Next, you must locate sources that discuss the long-term effects of natural disasters on survivors. As you search, you come across four possibilities. Which one is a non-credible source?

   A. Helping Victims of Tragedy, book by Dr. Ronald Zupree, PhD, M.D.

   B. JFK School's PTA website, article posted by Ferris Johnson, PTA president.

   C. "Disasters, Dilemmas and Solutions," a journal article by the American Red Cross.

   D. A documentary film on the Federal Emergency Management Agency's website, a government agency.

4. Explain your answer for question 3.

   _____

   _____

5. Finally, your teacher said to use at least one source that contains first-hand evidence. You manage to locate an earthquake survivor online and a book that contains several interviews with natural disaster survivors. Which piece of evidence will you use and why?

   _____

   _____

   _____

   _____

   _____

   _____

WRITE IN YOUR OWN WORDS

Presenting information from another text in your own words is called paraphrasing. When you **paraphrase** and cite other people's work, you avoid **plagiarism**. Plagiarism occurs when you copy someone else's ideas and pass them off as your own.

Example of paraphrasing vs. plagiarism:

Original text:
"Also, while news reports warned people that tsunami waves would be about ten feet, the waves actually reached fifty feet."

Acceptable paraphrasing:
1. The tsunami waves were forty feet higher than what news reports predicted they would be. *(Why acceptable: It is completely rewritten.)*
2. The author states that in spite of reported warnings of "waves that would be about ten feet," when the storm hit, "the waves actually reached fifty feet." *(Why acceptable: It gives proper in-text citation and uses quotation marks.)*

Plagiarism:

News reports warned the people in the area **that the waves would** reach a height of **ten feet**, but **the waves** actually **reached fifty feet** in height.

Paraphrase the following sentences from "Tsunamis—Waves Without Borders."

1. *"Tsunamis have hit somewhere in the world almost yearly since the times of Ancient Greece, and even before they could be recorded."*

   _____

   _____

2. *"About 3,500 years ago, for example, a tsunami struck the island of Crete. Historians believe that this disaster is what led to the downfall of the Minoans, a complex civilization that lived there."*

   _____

   _____

   _____

3. *"The effects of earthquakes and tsunamis are undoubtedly hard to recover from, and are often long-lasting. It is very hard for people to go back to the normal affairs of life."*

_____

_____

_____

CONDUCTING RESEARCH

Use "Tsunamis—Waves Without Borders" to complete the following activity.

In the text, the author states that researchers have reported that Japan has the best emergency readiness programs for earthquakes and tsunamis. Do additional research on this topic. Use at least three sources. In the space provided, write down your notes and ideas from your research.

Source 1:   _____

_____   _____

_____   _____

_____   _____

Source 2:   _____

_____   _____

_____   _____

_____   _____

Source 3:   _____

_____   _____

_____   _____

_____   _____

After your research, think about the following question:

Why did Japanese seismologists fail to predict the magnitude of the earthquake and tsunami, even though they have some of the most advanced systems in the world? Do additional research on this topic, and combine the new information you find with the facts that you discovered above. Based on all of your research, how would you answer this new question?

_____

_____

_____

_____

_____

_____

_____

_____

_____

EXPAND YOUR KNOWLEDGE:

Be Prepared! Many schools regularly conduct fire and tornado drills so that everyone is prepared in case of an emergency. In like manner, preparing at home is just as important for an unexpected event.

- Visit the following site with an adult: www.dhs.gov/how-do-i/prepare-my-family-disaster
- Review the following: <u>Disaster Kit Contents, Family Communication, Family Emergency Plan, and Warning Systems and Signals.</u>
- Take notes, make a list, and write down the important action steps so that you and your family are prepared for times of emergency. Share your findings with all of your family members as you create an emergency action plan.

WRITE YOUR EXPLANATION

Research a natural disaster of your choice that has changed a specific area, community, or environment. Then write an explanatory or informative essay about the disaster. Make sure to do the following:

- Introduce the topic clearly and provide a preview of what will follow.

- Develop by using relevant details to back up your thoughts and ideas. You may include diagrams, charts, or tables if you choose.

- Use facts and concrete evidence, and be sure to cite your sources.

- Use a formal and objective tone, be consistent in your verb tenses, and use different transitional words and phrases to make your writing more interesting.

- Use domain-specific vocabulary where appropriate.

- Provide a concluding statement that brings everything together and supports your explanation.

- Create a list of the sources you used for your research.

- Use in-text citations, where appropriate.

The March 11 earthquake generated a devastating tsunami that was observed all over the Pacific and caused tremendous devastation locally, including an accident at the Fukushima Daiichi Nuclear Power Plant.

Use the following chart to help brainstorm ideas for your essay.

Introduction: _____

_____

_____

Claim 1: _____   Supporting Details: _____

_____   _____

_____   _____

_____   _____

Claim 2: _____   Supporting Details: _____

_____   _____

_____   _____

_____   _____

Claim 3: _____   Supporting Details: _____

_____   _____

_____   _____

_____   _____

Conclusion: _____

_____

_____

Animals and People of the World

Animals and people may face different challenges depending on where they live. This unit discusses how some animals have adapted to their environments and continue to survive in their natural habitats, even though climates are changing. It also discusses some of these challenges including hunting, extinction, global warming, and lack of resources. You will also learn about special people who have made outstanding efforts to save endangered animals and to rebuild damaged areas of our home, the Earth.

Note: The references to authors, articles, and websites are purely fictitious in this workbook. These have been added to help students recognize, classify, and understand the different types of source material and how to assess if it is credible or not, as some of the Common Core Standards require.

Australia's Lightweight Champions

1 For most people, the word *kangaroo* creates an image of a fun, awkward-looking creature bouncing up and down in large plains. Kangaroos are pictured in films, books, video games, and popular cartoons such as *Winnie the Pooh*. Most people know that kangaroos are found in Australia. Some people may also know that kangaroos are herbivores, meaning they have a plant-based diet. Most people, however, may not know that kangaroos can stand at around six feet tall, making them the tallest of all marsupials, a class of animals that carry their young in a pouch, or that they have strong hind (back) legs, and even more powerful tails! Their legs and tails enable them to do things like leap as far as thirty feet in one jump, travel more than forty miles per hour, and protect themselves in the wild.

2 Kangaroos live in groups of ten to a hundred or more, known as courts, herds, troops, or mobs. Kangaroos belong to the animal family *Macropus* or *Macropodidae*, which means "big foot." Even though kangaroos develop enormous hind legs later in life, at birth they weigh about an ounce, the size of a grape or a honeybee. After birth, baby kangaroos, or joeys, find their way to their mothers' pouches and live there until they are able to survive on their own, usually at around ten months.

3 Shortly after they leave the comfort of their mothers' pouches, joeys learn that they have a few predators, including humans and dingoes, or wild dogs, and must learn how to protect themselves. Thanks to their steady feet and large tails, which provide them with support and balance, mature kangaroos are able to defend themselves from their natural enemies.

4 One way kangaroos protect themselves is by pounding the ground with their feet to demonstrate their power. When they feel threatened, they usually square up and box with their short front legs, and kick their opponent with their hind legs. One kick by a kangaroo's hind legs can severely injure the opponent. The kangaroo's ability to cause such great harm is a result of the power in their legs and the sharp claws on their feet. A kangaroo might also hiss, grunt, or make clicking noises to alert other kangaroos that the mob may be in danger.

Mother with joey in her pouch.

Interestingly, male kangaroos also box with each other to show that they are superior to other males; this is a survival skill that helps them stay alive and also helps them to find a mate.

5   Another way kangaroos survive is by using their tails. Recently, researchers at a university in New South Wales, Australia, reported that a kangaroo's tail serves as its fifth leg. This "fifth leg" is stronger than the animal's front legs and as powerful as a similar-sized human leg. Researchers knew previously that the kangaroo's tail is important to its movement, and is made up of strong muscles. However, they did not know that a kangaroo's tail helps it to walk and to conserve, or save, energy. The researchers found that when a kangaroo is walking, it uses its tail to lift both its hind and front legs. The tail also helps the body to move forward.

Kangaroos often use their tails as a fifth leg.

Digging Deeper

Boxing Kangaroos!
Kangaroos protect themselves and the rest of the mob by boxing. They also box each other as a way to show how strong they are during mating season. To see some kangaroos in action, visit the following website: *http://video.nationalgeographic.com/video/worlds-deadliest/deadliest-kangaroo?source=searchvideo*

CENTRAL IDEAS, KEY DETAILS, AND SUMMARIES

Use "Australia's Lightweight Champions" to answer the following questions.

1. Which statement best reflects the **central idea** of the text?

   A. Kangaroos mostly live in Australia and New Guinea, and are the tallest marsupials.

   B. Even though kangaroos box their opponents, the males also box each other during the mating season.

   C. Kangaroos have powerful hind legs and an even stronger tail that helps them move around and survive.

   D. Some of the most complex mammals on Earth are kangaroos because of the way they protect their young.

2. How does the author introduce and develop the idea that kangaroos have powerful hind legs and tails?

   _____

   _____

   _____

   _____

   _____

   _____

3. Provide a short **summary** of the article "Australia's Lightweight Champions." Be sure to restate the central idea and its supporting details.

   _____

   _____

   _____

   _____

   _____

   _____

   _____

USING PUNCTUATION CORRECTLY

A nonrestrictive element is a word, phrase, or dependent clause that provides added information, which is not necessary to a sentence. You may use dashes or commas to separate a nonrestrictive element in a sentence, or to break up a sentence.

> **Examples:** The waiter described the dinner specials, salmon and roasted chicken.
>
> Mother said—unless I heard her wrong—that she was headed to the grocery store after work.

Use "Australia's Lightweight Champions" to answer the following question.

1. Which of the following correctly uses dashes to separate a nonrestrictive clause at the end of the sentence, or to break up the sentence from the text?
   A. Kangaroos are depicted—or shown—in films, books, video games, and popular cartoons such as *Winnie the Pooh*.
   B. Kangaroos are depicted or shown in films, books, video games, and popular cartoons—such as *Winnie the Pooh*.
   C. Kangaroos—are depicted—or shown in films, books, video games, and popular cartoons such as *Winnie the Pooh*.
   D. Kangaroos are depicted or shown in—films, books, video games, and popular cartoons—such as *Winnie the Pooh*.

Challenge: Rewrite the following sentences. Include parentheses, commas, or dashes to set off nonrestrictive or parenthetical elements.

1. "Most people however may not know that kangaroos can stand at around six feet tall making them the tallest of all marsupials a class of animals that carry their young in a pouch."

   _____

   _____

2. "Shortly after they leave the comfort of their mothers' pouches joeys learn that they have a few predators including humans and dingoes, or wild dogs, and must learn how to protect themselves."

   _____

   _____

   _____

Standard L.6.2.a

Home	About Me	Saving the Mountain Gorilla	Resources

Saving the Mountain Gorilla

By Jasper Adams, writer at *Animals, Animals Magazine*

Feb 2013 | **Meet the Mighty Mountain Gorilla!**

1 Have you ever seen a mountain gorilla? They are quite interesting to watch! Mountain gorillas are a subspecies or subgroup of the eastern gorilla that lives in Central Africa, mostly in the Virunga Mountains of Rwanda, Uganda, and the Democratic Republic of Congo. Others live in four national parks found in the area. Since their discovery in 1902, mountain gorillas have endured several threats that even human beings sometimes do not survive, including war, hunting, climate changes, and the destruction of their natural habitats. According to *National Geographic*, at one point, there were only about 700 mountain gorillas remaining on Earth! This means that they are almost **extinct** and must be protected. My name is Jasper Adams and I am committed to efforts to help save the mountain gorilla. I follow in the footsteps of Dian Fossey—leader and pioneer in this mission. It is my hope that after reading about mountain gorillas on my blog, you decide to join or support the cause in whatever way that you can.

Read all about mountain gorillas here at www.jaspersblogspot.net.

HEIGHT metres	
5000	
4000	
3000	
2000	
1000	
500	
200	
0	
BELOW SEA	

Where Mountain Gorillas Live

Virunga Mountains
Rwanda

Home	About Me	Saving the Mountain Gorilla	Resources

April 2013 | **Getting to Know Mountain Gorillas**

2 On my first encounter, I discovered that mountain gorillas are usually larger than life! The adult males tend to be about 100 pounds heavier than the adult females. Standing up to six feet tall, the male can sometimes tower over the average human. Female mountain gorillas give birth after about eight and a half months of pregnancy, and unlike their parents, baby mountain gorillas weigh only about four pounds. The babies depend on their mothers for most things, including transportation and food.

3 Mountain gorillas are typically classified (grouped) by age. Males permanently leave their homes when they are about eleven years old to attract females to join them. The table on the right presents information about these classifications.

4 Like their cousin, gorillas, mountain gorillas can climb trees, but are often found in groups of about thirty on the ground. A group of mountain gorillas is referred to as a troop or band. On average, they live for about thirty-five years in the wild before they pass away, but they can have a lifespan of up to fifty years. Most troops are made up of several females and their offspring, as well as some young males, and led by one dominant male, known as the silverback because he usually has a band of silver hair going down his back.

Classification of Mountain Gorilla

STAGE	AGE-GROUP
Infant	Birth to 3.5 years
Juvenile	3.5 to 6 years
Subadult	6 to 8 years
Blackback	8 to 12 years
Adult female	from 8 years onward
Silverback	From 12 years onward

May 2013 | ## Mountain Gorillas Threatened

Mountain gorillas have thick, dark, long fur to protect them from the cooler temperatures of mountain living. Most are used to living at heights of 8,000 to 13,000 feet (about 2,500 to 4,000 meters) above sea level. However, these gorillas are losing their homes to people. As humans have moved further into the mountain areas, these creatures have been forced to move even higher up into the mountains, where they must deal with much colder temperatures than they are used to. These conditions are dangerous for the mountain gorillas and have contributed to their decreasing numbers.

5   In addition to losing their homes to humans, mountain gorillas have also had to deal with threats from hunters, disease, and war. For instance, local families harvest charcoal in the mountains where the gorillas live as a source for fuel for cooking and heating, although this practice has been banned. Nevertheless, people ignore this law and continue to do it. As a result, some of the mountain gorillas' habitat has been destroyed.

6   Mountain gorillas can be harmed by human disease. Therefore, it is sometimes unwise for them to come in contact with human beings. These animals cannot only catch human illness; they experience the sickness to a greater degree than do humans. A minor sickness like the common cold, for example, can kill a mountain gorilla.

7   Finally, during the Rwandan wars in the 1990s and the civil wars in the Congo, refugees (people seeking safety and shelter) fled into the mountains where the gorillas lived and took over their habitats. War rebels have also been known to take over the national parks where these creatures live and have killed some of the rangers who watch over them.

June 2013 | ## Hope for the Mountain Gorilla

8   Several researchers and organizations have been working for a long time to protect mountain gorillas. Scientists like Dian Fossey, for example, moved to Rwanda to learn more about them and to ensure that their habitats were intact. In addition, some organizations are working to ban hunting practices, especially in protected areas where mountain gorillas may live. Because of the many measures that have been put into place to make sure that mountain gorillas are protected, their numbers may be increasing slowly, though they still face major threats.

For more information on the different ways that you can get involved and support this cause, please contact jasper@savingmountaingorillastoday.com

Expand Your Knowledge:

Taking Action!
To learn more about efforts to save mountain gorillas, read more by visiting the following website:
www.awf.org/wildlife-conservation/mountain-gorilla

COMBINING IDEAS

Use the information and tables from the web page "Saving the Mountain Gorilla" to answer the following questions.

1. At which stage are male mountain gorillas when they leave their home in search for females? Explain your answer.

    _____

    _____

    _____

2. How old is the silverback when he typically becomes the leader of a troop? Explain your answer.

    _____

    _____

3. In what part of the country are the Virunga Mountains located in Rwanda?

    _____

4. How many meters above sea level are the Virunga Mountains according to the map?

    _____

5. Volcanoes National Park is located between which countries?

    _____

HYPERBOLE

Figure of Speech: A word or phrase that has a meaning different from what it actually means.
    Examples of figures of speech include **hyperbole**. A hyperbole uses extreme exaggeration to get the point across.

> Example: That mountain gorilla is older than dirt!

Use "Saving the Mountain Gorilla" to answer the following question.

1. Which of the following is an example of a **hyperbole**?
    A. Mountain gorillas are usually larger than life.
    B. Standing at about six feet tall, the male can tower over the average human.
    C. For the first two to three years of their lives, they cling to their mothers, leaving the nest to play with other mountain gorillas.
    D. On average, they live for about thirty-five years in the wild before they pass away, but can have a lifespan of about fifty years.

DENOTATIONS AND CONNOTATIONS

Denotation: The literal meaning of word; what a word actually means.
Connotation: The secondary meaning; emotional suggestions associated with a word.

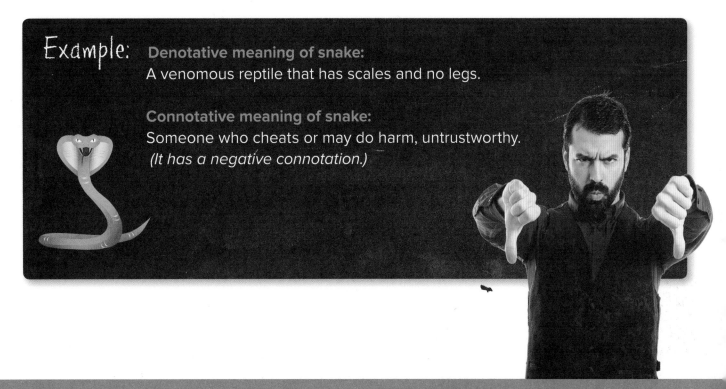

> Example: Denotative meaning of snake:
> A venomous reptile that has scales and no legs.
>
> Connotative meaning of snake:
> Someone who cheats or may do harm, untrustworthy.
> *(It has a negative connotation.)*

Use "Saving the Mountain Gorilla" to answer the following questions.

2. Read the following sentence:

    During the Rwandan wars in the 1990s, refugees took **shelter** *in areas considered to be* **home** *to the mountain gorillas.*

    A. What are the denotative meanings for the words **shelter** and **home**?

    _____

    _____

    B. Now, what is the connotative meaning of the word **home**?

    _____

    _____

3. Read the following sentences:

    Even though he is old, Jambo is a very **youthful** *mountain gorilla.*
    Even though he is old, Jambo is a very **childish** *mountain gorilla.*

    A. What are the denotative meanings for the words **youthful** and **childish**?

    _____

    _____

    B. Which sentence about Jambo has a *negative* connotation?

    _____

    C. Is the connotative meaning of the word **youthful** *positive* or *negative*?

    _____

    D. What is the connotative meaning of the word **youthful**?

    _____

    _____

Making Friends with Mountain Gorillas— Following the Footsteps of Dian Fossey

An Interview with Sandisha Coburn, by Farnsworth Henley

Primate Magazine, *April 2013 Issue*

Dian Fossey with one of her beloved gorillas. Photo courtesy of The Dian Fossey Gorilla Fund International.

Dian Fossey was a primatologist (a scientist who studies mammals such as chimpanzees and gorillas) who studied the great mountain gorilla. She was committed to saving the mountain gorillas from extinction and tried to persuade the public that these creatures are not as scary as was once thought. Several times, Fossey appeared in pictures playing with mountain gorillas, which helped to demonstrate that these giant animals could exist peacefully with human beings. Fossey's great discoveries about mountain gorillas included the social structures that dictate how mountain gorillas live, details about the gorilla diet, and learning that female mountain gorillas move from group to group over the years, rather than staying with one group over the span of their entire lives. She also learned about mountain gorilla speech patterns, also known as vocalizations. Dian Fossey has been compared to the likes of Jane Goodall, another primatologist and animal rights activist who studied chimpanzees in Tanzania.

In the January 1970 issue of *National Geographic*, Fossey wrote an article called "Making Friends with Mountain Gorillas." In that same year, famed scientist Sandisha Coburn, after reading the article, decided to follow in her footsteps. After much effort, I caught up with Dr. Coburn. Here is our interview.

Mr. Henley: How long have you been living in the mountains of Central Africa, studying mountain gorillas?

Dr. Coburn: It's been about three years. For three years, I have lived in the dense forests of the Virunga range, with eight volcanoes, some of the people of Rwanda, Uganda, and the Democratic Republic of Congo, and the gorillas. This has been our home.

Mr. Henley: Describe your experiences with the mountain gorillas. Are they as fiercely wild as we have seen in movies?

Dr. Coburn: I have become quite friendly with these creatures. Personally, I know them as individuals. I have given them names like Icarus and Uncle Bert, and they accept me. They typically travel in groups, and several of the groups know me and accept me as one of them.

Mr. Henley: How difficult was it to develop this kind of relationship with non-humans?

Dr. Coburn: Well, it surely was not easy at first. You see, scientists like myself are often told to sit and observe creatures, rather than to engage them. I thought it would be strange for them to have a foreign object just staring, so I copied some of their feeding and cleaning habits, and imitated the noises they made when communicating with each other.

Mr. Henley: You seem to have quite a love for these strange creatures. Tell us more.

Dr. Coburn: Mountain gorillas are actually not that strange at all. In fact, they are as smart as humans! Often, they have come close enough to observe my camera straps and my shoelaces. They have been studying me as much as I have been studying them.

Mr. Henley: You have been studying mountain gorillas for a while now and have been outspoken about their rights and protecting them from extinction. Can you share some of those experiences with us?

Dr. Coburn: The first mountain gorilla with which I developed a close friendship was Lolo. When I first arrived at Mount Visoke, a camp at which I would be doing different studies and collecting lots of data, I asked for one of my rooms to be turned into a forest. Though it was a strange request, some of the workers were used to my weird ways, and prepared one of the rooms as a forest like I had asked. Lolo had been captured for a European zoo, even though the habitats in which he lived were protected. I asked the Rwandese men to bring him to me until they were ready to ship him away, so I could nurse him and make sure he was healthy. Prior to coming to me, Lolo had been eating meals that were foreign to his diet and had a healthy fear of humans. Soon after he arrived, Lolo was joined by Parker, a female mountain gorilla who was in a similar position as Lolo. I would take the two gorillas into their natural habitats in the mountains and watch them as they played, fed themselves, and "spoke" with each other. This experience, along with others, stuck with me because I thought no human or animal should have to live caged up and in fear.

Mr. Henley: What happened to Lolo and Parker?

Dr. Coburn: Lolo and Parker were eventually shipped off, although I protested and did not want them to go. A couple of days after they had been taken away, I went back to the groups I had been observing, armed with notes and lessons learned from Lolo and Parker.

Mr. Henley: Is there anything in particular that stands out about these creatures that you think the world might not know?

Dr. Coburn: Like you mentioned before, the movies show the wild side of gorillas, but in reality, after about two thousand hours of observing them, I probably have five minutes of behaviors I would call wild or aggressive. Even so, these types of behaviors were expressed when the males were trying to protect themselves from situations in which they sensed harm or felt threatened; for instance, when they were being hunted. The Parc des Volcans in Rwanda, where I collected much of my data, was filled with hunters, poachers, and herdsmen who would walk their cattle right through the park even though this was illegal. Anyone would feel threatened in a situation like that! The poachers were especially a problem because they would set traps for other animals, which often hurt the gorillas. Some of these issues have contributed to the near extinction of mountain gorillas.

Mr. Henley: How do you think some of these problems can be solved?

Dr. Coburn: Money alone cannot solve everything. Politicians, conservation groups, and people who care must get involved, spread awareness about the issue, and put policies and laws in place to help protect the remaining mountain gorillas. I hope that some of my friends, Icarus, Uncle Bert, and Rafiki, amongst others, are still alive when help finally arrives.

Mr. Henley: Thanks for sitting down with me, Sandisha. Your work is inspiring to us all! It is helping to humanize these creatures that have, for so long, been seen as beasts.

Dr. Coburn: Yes, they are truly remarkable creatures! Beauties, not beasts!

Digging Deeper

Dian Fossey spent years of her life learning about mountain gorillas. Visit the following site to watch a video about her experiences: *http://video.nationalgeographic.com/video/short-film-showcase/mountain-gorillas-survival-dian-fosseys-legacy-lives-on*

DIFFERENT WAYS TO EXPRESS THE SAME IDEA

Sometimes, different authors might present information on one topic in different ways. The unique way in which information is presented about one topic helps the reader determine what an author's point of view is. One question to ask yourself when reading is, "How does the author feel about the topic, and what does he or she say to show those feelings?"

Use "Saving the Mountain Gorilla" and "Making Friends with Mountain Gorillas" to answer the following questions.

1. Compare and contrast the two texts. How are the ways the authors present the subject the same and different? How does each writer demonstrate how he or she may feel about mountain gorillas?

   _____

   _____

   _____

   _____

2. Based on the scientist's interview, how does she feel about mountain gorillas?

   _____

   _____

   _____

3. Does the author of the first text have the same purpose as the author of the second text? Explain your answer.

   _____

   _____

   _____

Challenge: How does the scientist's work with mountain gorillas shape the information presented in the second text? Does the author of the first text have the same point of view?

   _____

   _____

   _____

Wangari' Maathai—A Lady Like No Other

1 Green. Beautiful. Paradise. These words describe the African country of Kenya, where Wangari' Maathai was born. The country of her childhood was a lovely place full of lush green trees, wild animals, and large amounts of crops. Maathai was a very curious young girl with a strong love for learning, bound for great adventures. She had the privilege of attending school overseas and became the first East African woman to earn a doctorate degree. Upon returning back to her home country, Maathai was deeply disturbed by the deforestation problem in Kenya. The land was now barren; there were very few trees, so the crop and animal populations had decreased. Feeling the need to make a difference, Maathai decided to plant nine seedlings in her backyard. Soon, other women in her village were planting trees, and in time women throughout other parts of Kenya followed suit. Maathai spent most of her life showing the importance of taking care of the Earth. She accomplished this by demonstrating simple steps that people can take within their communities to have positive, far-reaching effects. Maathai's example has taught the value of hope and not giving up. As a result, she has become one of the most widely respected female **activists** in the world.

The Effects of Deforestation

2 The country of Kenya had been the victim of forest destruction for many years. In fact, a 1989 report from the **United Nations** (UN) stated, "on the African continent, on average only nine trees are planted to replace every 100 trees cut. The result of this magnitude of deforestation is soil **erosion** and water pollution, which, in turn interferes with animal nutrition and depletes firewood." Accordingly, Maathai noticed upon her return to Kenya the many women living in rural areas were having a hard time carrying out their daily chores. Walking several miles in search of firewood and lacking clean running water made tending the fields and being clean almost impossible. Furthermore, as Maathai conducted fieldwork, she confirmed that the loss of different species was the result of forest destruction. She also saw firsthand that soil erosion was a direct result of an environment existing without trees. Therefore, she was deeply moved to take action to save the Earth.

The Green Belt Movement

3 Moving on in her work, Maathai became the leader of the National Council of Women of Kenya (NCWK). In this position, she was able to enact a plan to carry out her life's mission. She stated in *Currents*, "The Earth was naked. For me the mission was to try to cover it up with green." In a **grass-roots** fashion, she began to spread the word. People were encouraged to plant trees that would actually form green belts of trees in what became her first campaign called *Save the Land Harambee*. *Harambee* is a Swahili word meaning "let's pull together." This is exactly what communities everywhere did. The campaign was a huge success, creating the Green Belt Movement (GBM).

Effects of the GBM

4 The GBM has had a major effect on society as a whole. Green Belt safaris were started to help create income for the GBM. Field trips and longer visits were arranged for travelers with the goal of providing firsthand educational experiences to exchange students in conservation and caring for the land. The students are taught the Green Belt Method of cultivating, planting, and caring for seedlings. The young people of Kenya no longer had to seek employment miles away from home in urban cities. They could stay in their rural communities, working in the GBM. They

Wangari' Maathai, winner of the 2004 Nobel Peace Prize.

learned how to care for the trees, and to advise on the progress and challenges that faced the program. Disabled young people who might otherwise have remained unemployed and forced to live in **squatter camps** were welcomed into the GBM, and given the fulfilling experience of doing what they could to care for the trees. Perhaps the most far-reaching effect is the Pan African Green Belt Movement, in which several other African countries have adopted the GBM vision along with an international division that had been established for countries outside of Africa. Using the Green Belt Method, these countries teach similar tree planting programs within their own communities.

5   What started as a small, local, woman-led organization has blossomed into a major economic **pillar** for the people of Kenya. Today, over 30,000 people have been employed by the GBM with over 5,000 nurseries and thirty million trees planted throughout the country. Many of these employed people are from rural communities with limited reading and writing abilities, who otherwise would not be able to support themselves or get the daily needs of life.

Remembering Wangari'

6   Maathai will always be remembered as a person who brought about powerful change in the world. Her work with the GBM provided a platform for her to get involved in additional activities. In 2002, she was elected to the Kenyan parliament. She directed the Kenyan Red Cross for eight years. Moreover, she has been granted over twenty awards for her work in education, health, and environmental issues, including the Nobel Peace Prize in 2004. According to *The New York Times*, former U.S. presidential candidate Al Gore said of her, "Wangari' overcame incredible obstacles to devote her life to service—service to her children, to her constituents, to the women, and indeed all the people of Kenya—and to the world as a whole."

glossary

Activist: A person who takes strong action on a side of a debatable issue.

Deforestation: Cutting down or burning all trees in an area.

Erosion: The process by which something is worn away.

Grass-roots: A basic level in an organization driven by common people who do not have a lot of money or power.

Pillar: A firm, solid upstanding part of society.

Squatter camp: A place where poor people live who cannot afford to live on their own.

United Nations: A governmental organization created to encourage cooperation among the countries of the world.

CENTRAL IDEAS, KEY DETAILS, AND SUMMARIES

Use "Wangari' Maathai—A Lady Like No Other" to answer the following questions.

1. Which sentence states the **central idea** of the text?
   A. Wangari' Maathai decided planting trees was the way to a better life for the people of Kenya.
   B. Wangari' Maathai is one of the most widely-respected female activists in the world.
   C. The Green belt movement created safaris and field trips as a source of income and education for the young people of Kenya.
   D. Wangari' Maathai's legacy includes helping physically disabled young people overcome obstacles so that they could become productive workers.

2. Which sentence from the text contains a **key detail** that supports the central idea?
   A. *"She had the privilege of attending school overseas and became the first East African woman to earn a doctorate degree."*
   B. *"Feeling the need to make a difference, Maathai decided to plant nine seedlings in her backyard."*
   C. *"Moreover, she has been granted over twenty awards for her work in education, health, and environmental issues, including the Nobel Peace Prize in 2004."*
   D. *"Furthermore, as Maathai conducted fieldwork, she confirmed that the loss of different species was the result of forest destruction."*

3. You have to prepare a two-minute report for class about a person who had a great and positive influence on the lives of others. You have chosen to write about Wangari' Maathai. **Summarize** the text in your own words, providing a good basis for this claim.

   _____

   _____

   _____

   _____

   _____

   _____

   _____

   _____

DETERMINING POINT OF VIEW AND PURPOSE

Every author has a purpose for writing and a point of view. Identifying the purpose of a text and locating important parts of the author's message will help you to read more effectively and increase your reading understanding.

Use "Wangari' Maathai—A Lady Like No Other" to answer the following questions.

1. What was the **author's purpose** for writing the text?

    A. To persuade or convince readers to join the Green Belt Movement

    B. To entertain readers with interesting facts about deforestation in Kenya

    C. To argue that Wangari' Maathai was one of the smartest women in Kenya

    D. To inform or teach readers about the work and achievements of Wangari' Maathai

2. Using evidence and details from the text, explain your answer to question 1.

    _____

    _____

EVALUATING AN ARGUMENT

Use "Wangari' Maathai—A Lady Like No Other" to answer the following questions.

1. What is one **claim** made in the text that supports the central idea?

    A. *The GBM became an economic pillar for the country of Kenya.*

    B. *Maathai conducted fieldwork to understand the loss of different species.*

    C. *Maathai helped to rebuild the country of Kenya, which had been the victim of forest destruction for many years.*

    D. *The youth of Kenya learned how to care for the trees, and to advise on the progress and challenges that faced the GBM.*

2. Which statement from the text provides the **best evidence** for the claim identified in question 1?

    A. *A 1989 report from the United Nations (UN) stated, "on the African continent, on average only nine trees are planted to replace every 100 trees cut…"*

    B. *"The students are taught the Green Belt Method of cultivating, planting, and caring for seedlings."*

    C. *According to The New York Times, former U.S. presidential candidate Al Gore said of her, "Wangari' overcame incredible obstacles to devote her life to service—service to her children, to her constituents, to the women, and indeed all the people of Kenya—and to the world as a whole."*

    D. *"The young people of Kenya no longer had to seek employment miles away from home in urban cities."*

3. Which sentence makes a claim that is **not** supported by information in the text?

   A. The country of Kenya was victim to forest destruction for many years.

   B. People were encouraged to plant trees and form "green belts" of trees all over Africa.

   C. Countries all over the world have adopted similar tree planting programs using the Green Belt Movement as a model.

   D. The Green Belt Movement has helped only a very small group of women in Kenya.

REFLEXIVE AND INTENSIVE PRONOUNS

Intensive Pronouns

- They emphasize (put special attention on) a noun or a pronoun already named.
- They usually appear right after the nouns or pronouns they are emphasizing.

Intensive pronouns are: myself, yourself, himself, herself, itself, ourselves, yourselves, and *themselves.*

Examples: Wangari' Maathai **herself** planted nine seedlings.
(herself emphasizes Wangari')

The president of Kenya **himself** made a speech about reforestation efforts.
(himself emphasizes the president of Kenya)

Reflexive Pronouns

- They refer to the subject of a sentence.
- In a sentence with a reflexive pronoun, the action of the verb reflects on the subject.

Examples: We bought seeds for **ourselves** and planted them in the front yard.
My brother planted the garden by **himself**.

Hint: To tell the difference between reflexive and intensive pronouns, just remember that reflexive pronouns do not emphasize anything. They just point back to or reflect the subject of the sentence.

In the following sentences, fill in the blanks with the proper pronoun. Then indicate whether it is an intensive or reflexive pronoun by putting an (I) or an (R) at the end of each sentence.

1. We _____ could not wait to plant new tree seedlings at our school.

2. Ava read to _____ about the life and accomplishments of Wangari' Maathai.

Standards L.6.1.b, RI.6.8

3. Rebecca _____ volunteered 10 hours a week at the Red Cross each week.

4. I _____ visited Kenya twice during the last three years.

5. The students took _____ on a self-guided tour of the rainforest.

WRITE YOUR ARGUMENT

Writing Tips
Do not use phrases like
"I feel,"
"I think that..."
"My thought is..."
These types of phrases will
weaken your argument.

The purpose of an argumentative essay is to *persuade* or *convince* readers about something you believe. Your claim should be supported by many pieces of evidence.

Imagine that you are a scientist working at the Earth-Animal-Fare Foundation. You have been working with mountain gorillas as well as engaging in reforestation efforts in countries that have been hardest hit by deforestation. Your organization has just received funding and must decide on which project to spend the money on for this year—more efforts to save the mountain gorillas, or efforts to replant the barren forest land in the Brazilian Amazon?

Your essay will be the deciding factor for the organization. Which project will you choose? Decide your stand and then write an essay arguing your view to persuade the panel to go with the project of your choice.

Why should more people get involved and save the animals? Why should all the money be spent on reforestation efforts in Brazil? Write an essay to support your argument, using evidence from the three texts, "Saving the Mountain Gorilla," "Making Friends with Mountain Gorillas," and "Wangari' Maathai: A Lady Like No Other," presented in this unit to support your claims.

Step 1: Introduce your claim—why should the organization of your choice receive funding? Gather evidence to present a well-rounded view of the topic. Use as many sources as you need to present enough evidence.

Step 2: Be prepared to address the opposing side of the argument to show that you have a broad understanding of the entire issue.

Step 3: Provide text-based facts, evidence, statistics, and reasons that support your position.

Step 4: Cite experts who agree with your claim.

Step 5: Use strong, decisive language (*According to latest research, Scientists have discovered, Studies have shown, Government reports show, and so on.*)

Step 6: Remember to be consistent with your style throughout your essay.

Step 7: Write a strong conclusion that restates your argument and sums up the reasons and evidence that will persuade your audience to follow your choice.

Use the following graphic organizer to help you arrange your thoughts.

My argument topic is:			
Reason 1	Reason 2	Reason 3	Reason 4
Evidence 1	Evidence 2	Evidence 3	Evidence 4
Fact 1	Fact 2	Fact 3	Fact 4

Conclusion: Wrap up your argument by writing a strong conclusion. Summarize the main points, evidence, and reasons supporting your argument.

Standards W.6.1.a–W.6.1.e

REVIEW

Valley of the Geysers

(Kamchatka Peninsula, Russia)

1 Geysers are wonderful sights to see that inspire awe. In fact, the Valley of the Geysers is one of the world's great wonders. Unfortunately, natural disasters and negative human behavior are responsible for events that have created environmental problems for geysers. As a result, some of the world's most beautiful wonders are in danger.

What Are Geysers?

2 Geysers are hot springs (with temperatures of about 199 degrees Fahrenheit /93 degrees Celsius) that force water and steam up into the air. They often develop around volcanic areas, where water leaks

into the ground and meets with heated rock. As this occurs, a type of constriction happens—an action that limits the water from flowing freely back to the surface. Because the water cannot easily get to the surface, heavy pressure builds and causes steam to form as the water is rising. It rises back to the surface escaping through the cracks. The heated water bubbles over and splashes in different directions, sometimes with force. This is the same kind of activity that causes volcanoes to erupt. As a matter of fact, some of the geysers shoot up in the air, much like lava exiting volcanoes.

3   There are only a few places in the world where geysers occur naturally—Yellowstone National Park in the United States, as well as in Chile, Iceland, New Zealand, and in the Kamchatka Peninsula near Siberia, Russia. A natural world wonder, the Valley of the Geysers in Russia is the second largest of its kind, attracting people from around the globe. Some of the largest geysers in the Valley of the Geysers can even shoot up to forty meters of overheated water into the air.

Geysers Threatened

4   Like many of the wonders in the world, the Valley of the Geysers has suffered damage over time as a result of changing climates, natural disasters, and human activity. On October 4, 1981, for instance, a **typhoon** caused a local river to flood, which pushed heavy rocks and boulders downstream. The combination of the overflowing river and boulders destroyed much of what was in its path. Moreover, this caused part of the geyser to collapse. About twenty-six years later, on June 3, 2007, another natural disaster occurred! This time, a landslide caused an entire mountainside to collapse. According to **conservationists** at the World Wildlife Fund, the landslide filled the Geyser River with millions of gallons of rock, snow, and ice. In trying to figure out what caused the landslide, scientists have discovered that Kamchatka is located in the "Ring of Fire," an area of the world where there are more than one hundred volcanoes. As a result, the ground underneath this area shifts often.

5   Additionally, scientists have studied the area and also discovered evidence that human activities such as tourism, **vandalism**, and the development of new cities and buildings have also affected the Valley of the Geysers. When people tour geysers, they may throw objects into the steam pits to see if water will erupt. While such behavior seems harmless, the water pressure and the steam's ability to move around can change, leading to changes in temperature and killing some of the small organisms that live in the geysers. The development of roads, buildings, and walkways have also harmed the geysers. Developers sometimes destroy parts of the land that surrounds the geysers in order to build new structures. While some of these structures may not affect the entire geyser, they are responsible for the destruction of certain sections of it.

Hope for Geysers

6   Organizations such as the World Wildlife Fund are committed to protecting these natural wonders and have suggested that the geysers be left alone so that these areas can heal. Scientists are also working with local governments to put policies in place that will protect the geysers and the wildlife that live near them. Together, we can make a difference in preserving these natural wonders!

glossary

Conservationist: A person who does work to protect the Earth.

Typhoon: A heavy rainstorm, often with high, strong winds.

Vandalism: The destruction of property on purpose.

Activity 1

Rewrite the following sentences using parentheses, dashes, or commas to set off nonrestrictive elements.

1. There are more geysers here in the United States at Yellowstone National Park than there are anywhere else in the world.

   _____

   _____

2. Cone geysers such as the Riverside Geyser erupt from a stream of water in a narrow cone.

   _____

   _____

Activity 2

Revise the following sentences from the passage so they are clearer. Make sure pronouns are in their proper cases (subjective, objective, possessive).

1. Because the water cannot flow freely to the surface, there is a lot of pressure and the water cannot boil. This causes steam to form when the water is rising.

   _____

   _____

   _____

2. The combination of the overflowing river and boulders was extremely powerful, and it destroyed much of what they found in their path.

   _____

   _____

3. On October 4, 1981, for instance, a typhoon (heavy, windy rains) caused a local river, the Gersenaya, to flood, which pushed heavy rocks and boulders downstream.

   _____

   _____

   _____

UNDERSTAND

Activity 1

Use "Valley of the Geysers" to answer the following questions.

1. Circle the letter of the sentence that contains the central idea of the text.

   A. The Valley of the Geysers in Kamchatka is the most impressive Wonder of the World.

   B. Because of natural disasters and human error, some of the Wonders of the World have been negatively affected.

   C. Human beings are the main reason why climates are changing and the world's wonders are being destroyed.

   D. At first, some human activities seem harmless, but in reality, all human activity has a big effect on the environment.

2. Where in the text does the author provide examples that show how severe weather has affected the Valley of the Geysers? Identify one of the examples in the space below. Use quotation marks around specific sentences or phrases cited directly from the text.

   _____

   _____

   _____

3. Though not directly stated in the text, what may have caused the landslide of 2007 in the Valley of the Geysers?

   _____

   _____

   _____

4. What evidence from paragraph 3 helps you draw that conclusion?

   _____

   _____

   _____

Activity 2

1. Which statement **best** describes why the author wrote this passage?
    A. To show the differences between geysers and other natural wonders
    B. To convince the reader to visit the Valley of the Geysers in Kamchatka Peninsula
    C. To argue that natural disasters are destroying all of the beautiful environments on Earth
    D. To inform the reader about the Valley of the Geysers and how natural events have changed it.

2. Describe the author's **point of view** about nature.

    _____

    _____

    _____

    _____

Activity 3

1. Which of the following is a **claim** that supports the main idea in the text? Circle the letter of the correct answer.
    A. Earth is filled with so many natural wonders, from pyramids, great walls, and geysers.
    B. Geysers are the result of what scientists call geothermic activity, which means the Earth is heating up.
    C. There are only a few places in the world where geysers occur naturally—Yellowstone National Park in the United States, as well as in Chile, Iceland, New Zealand, and in the Kamchatka Peninsula near Siberia, Russia.
    D. Like many of the wonders in the world, the Valley of the Geysers has suffered damage over time due to changing climates, natural disasters, and human activities.

2. Provide the best credible **evidence** from the text that supports the following claim:

    "Additionally, scientists have studied the area and also discovered evidence that human activities such as tourism, vandalism, and the development of new cities and buildings have also affected the Valley of the Geysers."

    _____

    _____

    _____

3. In the last paragraph, the author makes the following claim:

    "Organizations such as the World Wildlife Fund are committed to protecting these natural wonders and have suggested that the geysers be left alone so that these areas can heal."

    How does the author support this claim? Explain your answer.

    _____

    _____

    _____

    _____

    _____

    _____

Hot springs in the Valley of the Geysers, Kamchatka.

DISCOVER

What would you say? Let's take what you have learned and write about it!

Write Your Explanation

Throughout Units 4–6, you have learned about great biomes of the world, how weather patterns and climates have shaped different parts of the world and affected the species that live there, and the mystery that is nature! Over the course of history, scientists have studied these patterns in order to learn how to prevent natural disasters, provide us with warnings, and help us to successfully deal with issues such as global warming, which have negatively affected the Earth. It's your turn to pretend you are a scientist who studies weather patterns! Imagine that you are writing an article for a weather journal that explains the similarities and differences between the Valley of the Geysers in Kamchatka, Russia and the Amazon Rainforest.

Gathering Information

Step 1: Reread the articles "Amazon Rainforest" and "Valley of the Geysers."

Step 2: Ask an adult to help you search the Internet for more information on the Amazon Rainforest and the Valley of the Geysers in Kamchatka.

Hint: A good search engine to use is *www.google.com*, and you might use the phrases "Valley of the Geysers" or "Amazon Rainforest" in your initial search.

Step 3: Read the articles you locate and take some notes on the information you discover.

Hint: Focus on some larger topics such as climate, species, changing environmental conditions, or conservation efforts (measures taken to protect these natural wonders).

Step 4: Fill out the following Venn diagram, noting both the similarities and the differences between these two natural wonders.

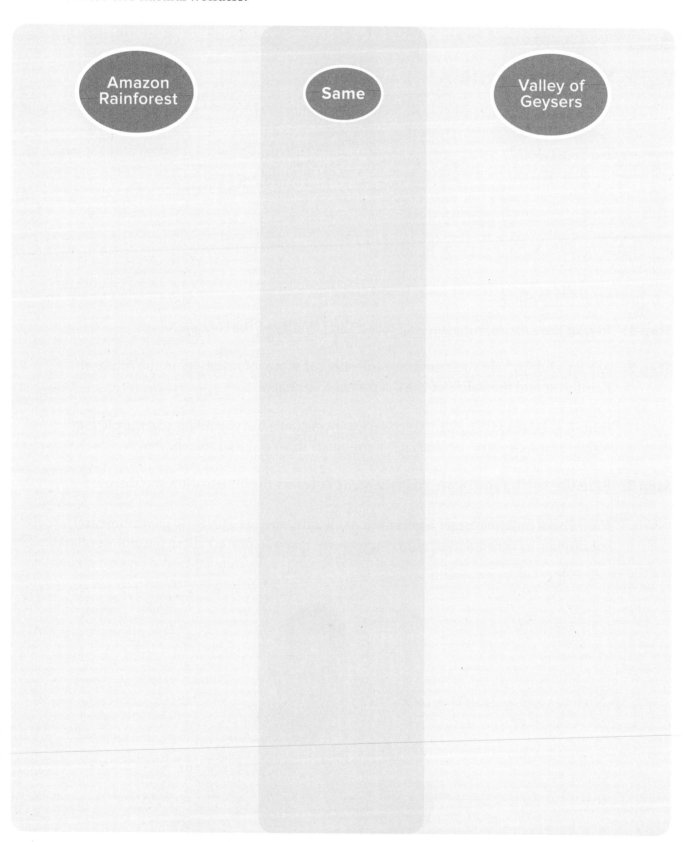

Amazon
Rainforest

Same

Valley of
Geysers

Standards W.6.2.a–W.6.2.f

Starting to Write

Step 5: Use the graphic organizer to arrange the information you found in your research and listed on your Venn diagram.

Claim: Write one or two sentences stating your central idea.

_____

_____

Central Idea 1:

_____

_____

Central Idea 2:

_____

_____

Central Idea 3:

_____

_____

Supporting Details:

1. _____

_____

2. _____

_____

3. _____

_____

Supporting Details:

1. _____

_____

2. _____

_____

3. _____

_____

Supporting Details:

1. _____

_____

2. _____

_____

3. _____

_____

Conclusion: Write one or two sentences to summarize your central idea and conclude the essay in a meaningful way.

_____

_____

Step 6: Take the information from your graphic organizer and write out your explanation (main points and details) in complete sentences. Be sure to include transition words and phrases to link your ideas!

Transition Words and Phrases You Might Choose To Use

for instance	also	in fact	for example	first	although
for this reason	in addition	however	therefore	finally	next

*Remember to use a comma after transition words that begin sentences!

Step 7: Ask an adult to read what you have written. Work together to do the following:

- Make sure you have presented three topics or areas in which there are similarities or differences between the Amazon Rainforest and Valley of the Geysers.

- Check to make sure your tone is more formal because you are writing for a textbook audience. Remove all instances of "I" and "you" from your essay.

- Look for places where you can make better word choices. Choose a few words from your essay and consult a thesaurus to see if you can choose better words to use.

- Proofread your paper for errors in grammar and mechanics.

- Pay special attention to commas with introductory elements and items in a series.

Hot springs in the Valley of the Geysers, Kamchatka.

Reading and Writing: Literature

In this section you will read stories, myths, and poems with amazing plots, interesting characters, and beautiful word pictures.

When you read literature, you gain a deeper understanding for things that are not easily understood. Literature explores strong emotions and related situations such as pain, love, and hate as well as human nature—both good and bad. By studying both positive and negative features of the human experience, little by little, you will gain a clearer picture of yourself and other people.

In the next few units, you also will learn just how powerful language can be. Word choice can imply much more information than what is directly being stated in a text. Literature can do this because it is multi-layered. The way something is said or written can appear to only express ordinary information on the surface, but in actuality, it speaks of conflict, sadness, jealousy, frustration, joy, deep love, mischief, and so on. When you study the use of language in this way, you can likewise learn how to use this technique for expressing language to your advantage.

When writing about literature, you will have to organize your thoughts and clearly state what you think and feel. As you write, new discoveries in your thinking will create connections to ideas and concepts that you already know. Working through what, at first, may seem challenging will open new pathways of learning, understanding, and communicating.

Folklore is a part of today's culture more than you may realize. It is defined as knowledge or communication that is passed down from person to person. Family traditions, holidays, and special sayings are all a part of folklore. It is often expressed in myths, fairy tales, stories, tall tales, rhymes, songs, and contains beliefs and customs stemming from a variety of traditions from different cultures.

Anansi and the Gub-gub Peas
An African Folktale

1   One year, a master planted a large rolling field of gub-gub peas. When ripe, their color is a dewy, sparkling green just like small candy gumdrops and they taste delicious. The peas are so special that some say the harvest season loves them. You can hear the peas singing in the fall, when the wind rustles against the ripe pods. In order to protect his gub-gub field, the master hired a big, strapping watchman to stand guard. As it turned out, the watchman had never been taught how to read.

2   The master's crop grew so huge and lovely, that anyone who passed by the gub-gub field wanted them like a bear wants honey! Anansi, the spider, lived nearby. Each time Anansi passed the field, he could hardly fight the desire to eat those tender, juicy, sweet green peas. It was as if magnets were pulling him to the gub-gub peas and there was nothing he could do to stop them! So he begged and begged the watchman to let him have some. The watchman refused. Anansi scurried away feeling very depressed because he was not allowed to eat the delicious gub-gub peas.

3   Anansi quickly felt better when he thought of an idea. He got a bird's feather, some berry juice, and papyrus paper and wrote a letter. Anansi brought the watchman an envelope with the letter and said it was from the master. "Read it!" Anansi excitedly said.

4   The watchman replied, "The master knows that I cannot read, so why would he give this to me?"

5   Anansi was puzzled. "Really? In that case, I will read it for you," Anansi said quite happily. "Hear this important message! The master wrote that you should tie me up in the middle of the gub-gub field so that I may feast on the peas, and when my belly gets full, only then should you let me go."

6   Anansi was so eager to take a whopping mouthful of peas that he could barely stop his tongue from draping over his bottom lip. Without delay, the watchman followed the instructions in the letter, and when Anansi ate his fill, he called to the watchman, who untied him and let him go.

7   When Anansi had left, the master returned and asked the watchman what happened to the peas. The watchman told him that he followed his orders in the letter he had sent by Anansi. The master replied that he had not sent any letter and to not believe what a stranger may say. He ordered the watchman that if anyone came back again saying this, he should tie him up in the field again, but this time, not let him go until he, the master arrived.

8   The next day, Anansi returned with the same letter, claiming it was from the master. He read it again to the watchman. At first, the watchman ignored Anansi because he was tired of his foolish tricks. But Anansi was so pushy that the watchman eventually tied him up in the pea field, and allowed Anansi to eat until his belly was ready to burst. Then he called to the watchman to let him go. But this time, the watchman said, "No, you can't go! Not this time!"

9   Being quick to think on his feet, Anansi claimed to have magical powers and said: "If you don't let me go, I'll spit on the ground you are standing on and you will rot away!" The watchman's face turned white as ash because he was very frightened, so he untied him and off Anansi went.

10   A few minutes later the master came by and learned what had happened. So again, the master ordered the watchman, "If Anansi returns tomorrow, pay no attention to his words, and do not let him go!" The next day, Anansi came back with his same trick. He read the letter to the watchman,

was tied up in the field, and ate until he was full. But this time, the watchman did not let him go.

1 The master finally returned and carted Anansi off to his yard and tied him to a tree until he decided what should be done with him. After thinking it over, he announced Anansi's punishment. He sentenced Anansi to five years of pulling and eating weeds from the gub-gub field. Anansi would not be allowed to eat anything else during those five long years.

2 Upon hearing his fate, Anansi became worried and cried a pool of crocodile tears. Just then, Lion walked by and stopped because he felt sorry for Anansi. "What is the matter?" asked Lion. Seeing that he had an audience, Anansi cried even louder and made up a big story. Lion felt even more sorry for him, and offered to take his place.

Lion untied Anansi and Anansi tied Lion up instead. Then, he quickly took off far into the bush and climbed a great tree as tall as a mountain so that he could look down to see what would become of Lion.

3 When the master returned to take Anansi to the field to begin weeding, he saw Lion. Not knowing what has happened, he decided that Lion could do the work in place of Anansi. After pulling his first row of weeds, Lion became tired and decided the work was just too hard. So he jumped up, broke the rope that was holding him and charged off into the bushes. The master was so upset that he sent out his best men to bring Lion back. After he ran for a while, Lion finally found the tree that Anansi was hiding in. He happened to see a golden leaf sparkle in the sun. It was barely covering Anansi's hind legs, and was so bright and shiny that it practically screamed the fact that Anansi was there. Excited to see Anansi, Lion called for him to come down. Instead, Anansi shouted cunningly, "See here! It's Lion, the one you are looking for! He is underneath the tree by the watering hole!"

4 Hearing this, Lion ran faster than the speed of light, into the bushes where he still is today, and Anansi got away free.

glossary

Gub-gub peas: A pale variety of peas from the black eye pea family, but with a white spot.

CENTRAL IDEAS, KEY DETAILS, AND SUMMARIES

Use "Anansi and the Gub-gub Peas" to answer the following questions.

1. What is the **central idea** or **theme** of the article?

    A. You do not need to know how to read to have a job.

    B. If you keep on trying, you may succeed in getting what you want.

    C. If you help someone, you may not always be thanked for what you did.

    D. A true friend will always help you, even if it means that he or she will hurt himself or herself.

2. Choose **two details** from the story that support the theme. Write your sentences on the lines provided.

    _____

    _____

    _____

    _____

3. Why was it was important for the author to include the detail about the watchman not being able to read. How does this relate to the theme of the story?

    _____

    _____

    _____

4. How does Lion respond at first when he sees Anansi crying?

    A. Lion gets mad at the master and helps Anansi create a new plan.

    B. Lion wants to eat the gub-gub peas too, so he takes Anansi's place.

    C. Lion feels bad for Anansi so he agrees to take the punishment from master.

    D. Lion decides that he likes to eat weeds and volunteers to take Anansi's place.

5. How does Lion change, and what finally happens to him because of his decision to try to help Anansi?

    _____

    _____

    _____

    _____

UNDERSTANDING FIGURATIVE LANGUAGE

When authors write in words or phrases that mean something other than their literal definitions, they are using figurative language. There are different types of figurative language, which you'll learn about throughout the following lessons.

Hyperbole is the use of exaggerated terms and words to make a point.

> Example: We jumped for joy when we saw **the boatload of food** available at the buffet.

Imagery is the use of language to create visual pictures of ideas in our mind that awakens our physical senses.

> Example: The **sweet smell of cinnamon spice** coming from the baking apple pie made my mouth begin to water.

Use "Anansi and the Gub-gub Peas" to answer the following questions.

1. Read the following sentence. Tell whether this is an example of hyperbole or imagery.

   *"Hearing this, Lion **ran faster than the speed of light**, into the bushes where he still is today..."*

   Type of figurative language: _____

   What does **ran faster than the speed of light** mean when it is used to describe the lion?
   A. The lion was very scared.
   B. The lion was able to run faster than normal.
   C. The lion was able to run faster than Anansi.
   D. The lion was uncertain if he should run at a normal speed.

2. Read the following sentence:

   *"Upon hearing his fate, Anansi became worried and cried **a pool of crocodile tears**."*

   Type of figurative language: _____

   What is the best meaning of the phrase **a pool of crocodile tears**?
   A. A lot of sad tears
   B. A lot of fake tears
   C. A lot of happy tears
   D. A lot of unusual tears

UNDERSTANDING PERSONIFICATION

Personification, another example of figurative language, gives human qualities to an object or animal. Authors use personification to make stories more dramatic and interesting.

Examples: My car **was thirsty** for more gas.
The frame **felt lonely** without a picture.
Her poor drooping flowers **were begging** for the sun.

Use "Anansi and the Gub-gub Peas" to answer the following questions.

1. Which sentence from the story is an example of personification?
    A. "As it turned out, the watchman had never been taught how to read."
    B. "The peas are so special that some say the harvest season loves them."
    C. "Then, he quickly took off far into the bush and climbed a great tree as tall as a mountain."
    D. "The master's crop grew so huge and lovely, that anyone who passed by the gub-gub field wanted them like a bear wants honey!"

2. Read this sentence from the story:

    "He happened to see a golden leaf sparkle in the sun. It was barely covering Anansi's hind legs, and was so bright and shiny that it practically screamed the fact that Anansi was there."

    What is being personified in the sentence?_____

Challenge: Imagine that Lion refused to help Anansi. Write a paragraph or two showing a conversation between them. What did Lion say? What would have Anansi done? Include one example of hyperbole, one example of imagery, and have at least one example of something other than Lion or Anansi being personified.

_____

_____

_____

_____

_____

_____

Aladdin, the Magic Lamp, and the Princess
A Middle Eastern Folktale

1   A long time ago, a young man named Aladdin and his mother lived in a rural village in Asia. Aladdin's father died when he was just a very small boy, and because of that, Aladdin and his mother were quite poor. One night, just as Aladdin and his mother were about to eat their last piece of bread, there was an extremely loud pounding at the front door. It sounded like thunder inside their tiny house! "Please don't get up," Aladdin said to his mother, because he knew she was very tired from working so hard. "I'll find out who it is." Aladdin opened the door, and there stood a ferocious and fearsome looking fellow! He looked old, but strong, and seemed to come from a far-off land.

2   "Hello, Aladdin, it has been many years since we have met," said the man.

3   "I'm sorry sir, but who are you?" Aladdin asked. "I don't recall ever meeting you."

4   "Ah, but we have met, long ago," the man replied. "I am your father's brother, your uncle. I have been away for many years, and now I have come back, a famous magician." At that he began performing many tricks. Aladdin and his mother were impressed. They had never seen such magic before! Finally, the magician turned back to Aladdin.

5   "Come with me, young man," he ordered.

6   "But where are we going?" Aladdin asked.

7   "I am your uncle, and I will help you and your mother," the magician replied. "But first, you must come with me." The man was not truly Aladdin's uncle, and instead hoped to trick Aladdin into helping him. But Aladdin really believed that the magician was his uncle and could help his mother, so he agreed.

8   Aladdin followed the magician far outside the village. After walking for a time, they finally came to the opening of a cave. "Now my son," said the magician, "You must go into the cave. There will be a golden lamp inside. Bring it to me!"

9   Aladdin entered the cave. As he descended ever deeper into the dense darkness of its depths, he began to wonder if maybe there was no lamp, and it was a trap. Finally, he stumbled upon an old dirty lamp. "This must be it," he thought, and began returning to the surface. The way out of the cave was difficult, and Aladdin called to the magician.

10   "Please, Uncle, come and help me on these steep rocks!" "First give me the lamp," the magician said. "Then I will help you."

11   "No, help me first!" Aladdin replied, for he was beginning to worry that the magician was not who he claimed to be.

12   Suddenly, the cave was filled with a bright, glowing light and a genie appeared, seeming to come from inside the lamp!

13   "Who has called to me?" the genie said, his voice thunderous inside the cave walls. "What is your command?"

14   "Who are you?" Aladdin replied fearfully.

15   "I am the genie, the slave of the lamp. Whenever someone rubs the lamp, I appear to grant their every wish. You have rubbed the lamp. What is your command?" the genie repeated.

16   Aladdin could not remember rubbing the lamp, but assumed it must have happened when he fell. He was not about to turn down such an amazing opportunity. His thoughts immediately turned to his mother, and to his present problem of being stuck in the cave.

17   "Genie," Aladdin says, "I wish to see my mother, and for her suffering to end. I want you to give her a large, richly furnished house, the finest clothes money can buy, and all the food she could ever want."

18   Almost before he could finish speaking, Aladdin found himself back with his mother. Sure enough, their tiny house had been replaced by a grand residence filled with incredible riches, and his mother wore clothing fit for a queen.

19   Before Aladdin even had time to think about what he wanted his next wish to be, he heard noise coming from the streets and ran to the window to see the commotion. It was the royal musicians, playing a fanfare as they marched ahead of the sultan of the land. Next to the sultan was his beautiful daughter! Aladdin had secretly been in love with the sultan's daughter for years, but had always known that as the son of a poor widow he would never be an acceptable husband for a princess. Suddenly, he knew what his next wish should be. He rubbed the lamp quickly.

20   Again, the genie appeared. "I am here, master. What is your command?"

21   "Give me fine clothes, riches, and servants!" he demanded. Immediately, his wish was granted. He set off for the sultan's palace dressed as a prince, surrounded by servants carrying large baskets of riches. The sultan was impressed by Aladdin's wealth, and permitted him to come inside the palace. Once inside, Aladdin lost no time finding the sultan's daughter. He boldly confessed his love for her and asked for her hand in marriage.

22   "But I cannot," she replied. "I am promised in marriage to Mestikel, the son of the grand vizier." Aladdin knew that only something very serious would make the princess break her promise of marriage to Mestikel. He rubbed the magic lamp for the third time, and once again the genie appeared. "What is your command, my master?"

23   Aladdin asked the genie to help him show the sultan's daughter just what kind of man Mestikel really was. He had the genie put on a disguise and tell Mestikel that the sultan was upset with his daughter and had decided not to let her inherit.

24   "Why, if she has no money, I certainly do not want to marry her!" Mestikel replied. The sultan's daughter could see that Mestikel was a cruel and unkind man who did not love her, and told him that she would not marry him. Instead, she married Aladdin, who became the prince of the kingdom, and they lived happily ever after.

CENTRAL IDEAS, KEY DETAILS, AND SUMMARIES

Use "Aladdin, the Magic Lamp, and the Princess" to answer the following questions.

1. Which sentence best describes the **central idea** of the story?

    A. Aladdin and his mother are poor and need more to eat.

    B. Aladdin gets to meet his uncle for the first time.

    C. Aladdin finds a lamp with a genie inside who grants his wishes.

    D. Aladdin has been in love with the sultan's daughter for a long time.

2. What **two details** would be important to include in a summary of the article?

    _____

    _____

    _____

3. The author includes the detail that the magician has Aladdin go into the cave to find the lamp. Why is it important to the events of the story that Aladdin finds the lamp instead of the magician?

    _____

    _____

    _____

4. How does the magician react when he finds out that Aladdin is not going to give him the lamp, and how does that affect Aladdin?

    _____

    _____

    _____

5. What helps the sultan's daughter see that Mestikel is not a good person to marry? Cite specific evidence from the text to support your answer.

    _____

    _____

    _____

UNDERSTANDING ALLITERATION

When a series of words in a row, or close to a row, have the same beginning sound when you say them, this is called alliteration. You can identify alliteration by sounding out a sentence and then looking for words in the sentence with the same sounds.

Examples: Suzie sells seashells by the seashore.
Hank's home hopefully has heat!
Carly's cat clawed her couch, causing her to cry.

Use "Aladdin, the Magic Lamp, and the Princess" to answer the following questions.

1. Which sentence or phrase from the story is an example of **alliteration**?
    A. "The sultan was impressed by Aladdin's wealth, and permitted him to come inside the palace."
    B. "Aladdin could not remember rubbing the lamp, but assumed it must have happened when he fell."
    C. "In his anger, he hurled a large rock at the entrance of the cave, sealing it shut…"
    D. "As he descended ever deeper into the dense darkness of its depths…"

2. Which words from the sentence you chose make the sentence alliterative?
    Write your answer on the lines provided.

    _____

    _____

3. Cite two additional sentences from the story that are examples of alliteration. Write the sentences on the lines provided.

    _____

    _____

    _____

    _____

Challenge: Write your own alliterative sentence using at least one character from the folktale.

    _____

COMPARING MEDIA

Use "Aladdin, the Magic Lamp, and the Princess" to answer the following questions.

1. In the story, what kind of man is Mestikel? What do you know about him based on the text? How do you feel about him as a character? Write at least two sentences describing Mestikel.

_____

_____

_____

_____

2. Describe how you pictured the magician in your mind as you read the story. Is he nice? What does he look like? How does his voice sound when he speaks to Aladdin? Write at least two sentences that describe the way you imagined him based on the information in the text.

_____

_____

_____

_____

3. Think about the genie in the story. How does he make Aladdin feel when he appears from the lamp? How does he move around? Is he big or small? Is he scary or kind? Write at least two sentences that describe the way you pictured the genie in your mind as you read the story.

_____

_____

_____

_____

Visit the following website to watch the video version of "Aladdin and the Magic Lamp."
https://archive.org/details/Aladdin_315

After watching the video, answer the following questions:

4. What are the differences that you notice in the way you picture the story version of Mestikel, and the video version of him? Does one source give you more information about the character? Write at least two sentences that describe the difference between the story version of Mestikel and the video version of him.

_____

_____

_____

_____

5. Think about the details the video gives you about the magician. What differences do you notice in how he is described in the story and how you see him in the video? Think about both his character and his appearance. Write at least two sentences that contrast the way you pictured the magician as you read the story and the way you saw him in the video.

_____

_____

_____

_____

6. Now think about the way you pictured the genie in the story. How is he different in the video? In two sentences or more, describe the way that the genie is different in the video from the way you pictured him in the story.

_____

_____

_____

_____

WRITE YOUR NARRATIVE

Now it's your turn to write your own folktale! Use your imagination to create an interesting story. Pick a theme, characters, and a plot. What will you write about?

Step 1: Identify your theme.

Step 2: Create your characters. What are their names? What are they like? Describe this character—how old is he or she? What is special about this character?

Character 1

_____

_____

Character 2

_____

_____

Character 3

_____

_____

Character 4

_____

_____

Step 3: Tips when writing:
- Use dialogue between your characters to develop the events within the story.
- Use transition words, phrases, and clauses to signal shifts in time or settings.
- Use descriptive language. What are the smells? Sights? Tastes? Write to appeal to the five senses.

TRANSITION WORDS AND PHRASES			
in addition	again	now, until now	therefore
furthermore	next	at length	in other words
Further	finally	this time	after all
moreover	once	so far	in contrast
first	sometimes	nearby	otherwise
second, secondly	following	wherever	accordingly
last, lastly	in the meantime	because	as a result
but	however	in like manner	nevertheless

Step 4: Start to write:

Use the graphic organizer to arrange the material for your story.

Topic: Write one or two sentences about your main idea.

_____

_____

Establish your plot. What happens?

First	**Second**	**Third**
Supporting Details:	**Supporting Details:**	**Supporting Details:**
1. _____ _____ 2. _____ _____ 3. _____ _____	1. _____ _____ 2. _____ _____ 3. _____ _____	1. _____ _____ 2. _____ _____ 3. _____ _____

Conclusion: How does your story end? Write a few sentences to summarize your main idea and wrap up the story in a meaningful and exciting way.

_____

_____

_____

_____

Greek and Roman Myths

A myth is a traditional story that teaches a lesson, tells why something happened in the past, or explains the unexplainable in a way that people can understand. Often, myths have supernatural characters and events, such as gods and goddesses, spirits, monsters, curses, and transformations. Many groups of people have their own mythology, or set of related myths that are unique to their culture. One of the best preserved mythologies comes from the ancient Greeks and Romans. Although the ancient Greeks and Romans had different cultures, the time period and the location in which they existed sometimes overlapped, so their myths were often very similar, and they worshipped many of the same gods and goddesses. In this unit, you will use several well-known Greco-Roman myths to practice your reading, writing, and vocabulary skills.

The Sun Chariot

1 Long ago, there was a young boy named Phaethon who lived with his mother, Clymene. Now, Clymene was a human, but her son was only half-mortal, for his father was Helios, God of the Sun. Phaethon loved nothing more than to brag to his friends about the power and importance of his father. He would boast of how Helios, the fearless driver of the glowing gold chariot of the sun, rose every morning in the east and pulled the glorious light of day across the arc of the sky to its resting place in the west. Then he would tell of his father's strength, and how day after day, he guided the four wild horses needed to pull the magnificent chariot.

2 "It is thanks to my father, Helios, that all of you know the beauty of the day, and the peace of the night," Phaethon would say, "for it is only by his hand that the great steeds are kept in check, and the order of the heavens preserved."

3 Phaethon's companions soon tired of this boasting. Only Epaphus, though, was bold enough to confront the arrogant young half-mortal, for he, too, was the son of one of the Gods. "Why are you always boasting?" Epaphus said one day. "Helios is only your father in your imagination. You are no better than anyone else, and probably do not even know who your *real* father is."

4 Angered to the point of tears by the insult to himself and the accusation against his mother, Phaethon immediately ran to Clymene and demanded the truth. "Am I really the son of Helios? If I am, give me some proof, so that I can defend us to those who say otherwise!" he pleaded.

5   Clymene, too, was enraged by the accusations, for she had never loved anyone but the sun god Helios, and knew for certain that her son was the child of the god. "I swear to you," she replied, "by the sunlight you see here around us, which comes from the great god Helios, that you are truthfully his son. If I am lying, may he never allow me to see light again! Look, his palace is not far from here. You should go to it and visit him, and he will confirm the truth himself."

6   At once, young Phaethon set out for the palace of the sun. As soon as he arrived, though, he was struck with awe by the size and beauty of his surroundings, and could not bring himself to approach any nearer to the god, who was adorned with a brilliantly shining crown.

7   "Why have you come here, Phaethon?" Helios said, seeing the boy's nervousness.

8   "To find out if I am really your son, or whether my mother, Clymene, has been dishonest with me," Phaethon said, trembling as he spoke.

9   Taking pity on the boy, Helios removed his glowing crown. "Come here, my son," he said, "for Clymene has spoken the truth, and I am, indeed, your father." At that, the god hugged his half-mortal son, comforting him. Then he continued: "Yet, that you may have no doubt of the matter ever again, tell me what gift I can give you as a sign that what I say is true. Whatever you ask, I promise I will grant it to you."

10   Almost before the god could finish speaking, Phaethon blurted out the one request that had long been dearest to his heart. "Let me, O Father, guide the chariot of the sun across the sky for one entire day! For I am the son of the mighty Helios, and can surely succeed at this task!" Horrified by the boy's request, Helios immediately regretted his promise, and attempted to convince his son to forget his crazy and dangerous desire. "Anything but this, my son, I could surely do!" he exclaimed in panic. "But it is impossible for me to agree to this. The path is difficult, and the horses are unruly! Even the great Zeus, highest and most powerful of all the gods, is unable to control them! So how could a mere boy ever hope to lead them properly? You must ask me for something else."

11   But young Phaethon would not listen to the advice of his father, and instead kept pleading his case, insistent on driving the chariot of the sun.

12   Eventually, Helios gave up trying to convince the boy. "I have given my word, and so I must grant this request of yours, even though I wish with all of my heart that I could refuse you," he said. To protect his half-mortal son from the dangers of the sun's rays, he smeared a special potion on Phaethon's face, and placed the brilliant crown on the boy's head. With a few final words of advice, he stepped back and allowed his son to jump up into the grand chariot. "Be careful!" he said. "Stay on the path, never going to the right or the left, or you will surely burn the heavens and the earth with the great heat of the sun. Do not whip the horses, or treat them roughly, but be firm with the reins. In this way, you will have the best possible chance of success, even in this ill-advised plan."

13   As soon as the dawn signaled that the new day was beginning, Phaethon urged the horses to move forward. The horses, though, could sense that it was not Helios' practiced hands which held their reins, but those of an inexperienced child. Immediately, they rebelled, racing ahead and leaving their track entirely. In a panic at this turn of events, Phaethon could do nothing! The reins lay useless in his hands as the chariot veered this way and that. He began to wish he had never asked to drive the sun chariot.

14   The horses rushed through the skies, scorching the stars and the clouds as they passed. Then, they turned toward Earth, coming closer to her than ever before. Cities were destroyed as the sun blazed past. Rivers dried up, and the ground became dry and cracked wherever the sun came nearest.

15   Finally, the Earth cried out to Zeus, "Please, make this terrible thing stop! I am nearly ruined, and if you do not act soon, the heavens, too, will be destroyed!"

16   Zeus could see that the Earth was telling the truth, and called all the gods together, including Helios, who had allowed his son to take the chariot in the first place. "If I do not act," he said, "the Earth will be destroyed. I do not want to do this thing that I am about to do, but I must." At that, he formed a lightning bolt and hurled it toward the out of control chariot. The lightning bolt's great power halted the chariot's progress and stopped the sun's destructive fire. However, the shock of the lightning threw Phaethon from the chariot, and he fell down to the Earth, finally landing in the river Eridanus.

17   Phaethon was never seen again, and Helios grieved when he learned that his son was gone. For an entire day, the sun was not seen as the great god mourned. The other gods were also sad, but they eventually convinced Helios to return to his job, and even today, Helios rises every morning with the sun, carries it across the sky in his great chariot, and descends into the west at evening.

CENTRAL IDEAS, KEY DETAILS, AND SUMMARIES

Use "The Sun Chariot" to answer the following questions.

1. Which statement reflects the **main idea**, or **theme**, of the myth?
    A. When children fight with each other, the results can be deadly.
    B. Even a father's love is not strong enough to stop a child from making bad decisions.
    C. Pride and over-confidence often lead to disaster.
    D. When people work together, they can help someone that is feeling depressed.

2. While the myth of Helios and Phaethon certainly contains a moral, or lesson about human nature, it also tries to explain things that occur in nature. Identify two natural phenomena, or things that exist and occur in nature, that are explained by the myth. Be sure to include a brief summary of the explanation, that the myth gives.

    _____

    _____

    _____

    _____

    _____

    _____

    _____

EXPAND YOUR KNOWLEDGE:
Greek and Roman mythology have had an incredible amount of influence on our modern world. The more myths you read, the more names, places, words, and events you will find that you are already familiar with. Mythology pops up in popular books, movies, and TV shows—it even shows up on stamps (see image)! Check out this website, which compiles thousands of the mythology references from the world around us. Some will probably be familiar, but others may surprise you! http://greekmythologytoday.com/

CHARACTERS AND INFERENCES

In most stories, there are two kinds of characters: **static** characters and **dynamic** characters.

- A static character is one who remains the same throughout the story.

- A dynamic character changes throughout the story. Sometimes, the character becomes a better person or learns a lesson. Other times, the character changes for the worse. To readers, dynamic characters seem more interesting or may be more important to the main events of the story.

1. Think about the following characters from "The Sun Chariot," and decide whether they are **static** or **dynamic**. Indicate your answer by writing an "S" for "static" or a "D" for "dynamic" in the space provided next to each name.

   Zeus _____   Helios _____   Epaphus _____   Clymene _____   Phaethon _____

2. Pick one of the characters that you identified as dynamic and describe why that character is dynamic in the space below. (If you did not identify any characters as dynamic, explain why not.)

   _____

   _____

   _____

   _____

   _____

   _____

   _____

   _____

   _____

   _____

   _____

   _____

   _____

   _____

   _____

Standards RL.6.1, RL.6.2, RL.6.3

3. Which of the following **inferences** could a reader of this myth make?

   A. Epaphus was actually jealous of Phaethon, which was why he insulted him and his mother.

   B. Helios felt responsible for what happened to Phaethon because he let him drive the chariot.

   C. The Earth was exaggerating when she told Zeus that the heavens could be destroyed by the sun.

   D. Phaethon never really expected Helios to let him drive the chariot, which is why he panicked.

An **inference** is something that is not specifically stated in the text. By paying attention to the details, you can collect information to help you come to a conclusion.

4. By studying myths like "The Sun Chariot," people living today can find out what was important to the ancient Greeks and Romans, how they felt about the world around them, and more. What is one thing you can infer about Greek and Roman culture from reading "The Sun Chariot"?

_____

_____

_____

_____

_____

_____

_____

5. Which of the following statements about "The Sun Chariot" is a fact, not an opinion?

   A. Zeus knew that throwing the lightning bolt at the chariot would probably kill Phaeton, but he did it anyway because he thought it was necessary.

   B. Phaeton's death was actually Epaphus' fault, because if Epaphus had never insulted Phaeton and Clymene, Phaeton would never have ended up driving the chariot.

   C. Although Helios was a god, he was the weakest character in the myth, because he let himself be persuaded by his son, who was only half god.

   D. Zeus only decided to intervene and stop the chariot because the Earth pointed out that if he allowed it to continue, the heavens would be in danger.

MAKING WORDS

In English, many words have a **root**, or main "chunk" with a distinct meaning that the rest of the word is constructed on. **Affixes**, which also are word "chunks" with their own meanings, can be added, or "affixed," to the root or another word to make it more specific, or even turn it into a word with a completely different meaning. Some affixes are **prefixes**, and are added to the beginning of a word; others are **suffixes** and are added at the end. Many of the roots and affixes that we see in everyday words come from Greek and Latin languages. Consider a few examples (it may help to keep a dictionary nearby for any words you do not recognize):

Word Root	Meaning	Examples from English
astro	stars, heaven, space	**astro**naut, **astro**nomy
ped/pod	foot	**ped**estrian, **pod**iatrist
fac	to make, to do	**fac**tory, manu**fac**ture
Prefix	Meaning	Examples from English
pre-	before, earlier	**pre**mature, **pre**fix
non-	not, the absence of	**non**sense, **non**committal
ex-/exo-	out of, from	**ex**tract, **exo**skeleton
Suffix	Meaning	Examples from English
-al/-ial	related to, characterized by	logic**al**, topic**al**
-hood	state, quality, condition of	state**hood**, mother**hood**
-ly	in what manner	slow**ly**, crazi**ly**

Words can also be made up of multiple "chunks" that have been put together. For instance, consider these combinations of Greek and Latin prefixes, suffixes, and root words:

English Word	Word Meaning	Word Parts
Geology	The study of the earth	**geo** (root, "earth") **-ology** (suffix, "study")
Manuscript	A document written by hand	**man/manu** (root, "hand") **scrib/script** (root, "to write")
Interject	Suddenly say something, interrupt	**inter-** (prefix, "between, among, during") **ject** (root, "to throw")
Retractable	Able to be withdrawn or pulled back	**re-** (prefix, "again, back or backward") **tract** (root, "to pull") **-able** (suffix, "capable, susceptible")

By breaking the word down into its basic parts, or "chunks," and thinking about what each of the "chunks" mean, you may be able to figure out a basic definition for the word. Of course, you should always remember to use context clues, or details about what is going on in the text, too!

The following questions about root words and affixes use words found in "The Sun Chariot":

1. Read the following quote from the myth:

   "*But it is **impossible** for me to agree to this. The path is difficult, and the horses are unruly!*"

   What is the root of the word of **impossible**?

   _____

   What is the prefix that has been added to the root word?

   _____

   Based on your knowledge of the entire word, how would you define the prefix by itself?

   _____

   _____

2. Read this sentence from the myth:

"He would boast of how Helios, the fearless driver of the glowing gold chariot of the sun, rose every morning in the east and pulled the **glorious** *light of day across the arc of the sky to its resting place in the west."*

The suffix **–ious** most likely means:

A. state of being;

B. over, too much;

C. large, powerful; or

D. possessing, full of.

3. Read the following sentences from the myth:

"Then he would tell of his father's strength, and how day after day he guided the four wild horses needed to pull the **magnificent** *chariot"*

"To find out if I am really your son, or whether my mother Clymene has been **dishonest** *with me, Phaethon said, trembling as he spoke."*

"The lightning bolt's great power halted the chariot's **progress** *and stopped the sun's* **destructive** *fire."*

Based on your knowledge of the highlighted words, your knowledge of word roots and affixes, and the context clues in the sentences, match each word part with its meaning by writing the number of the correct answer in the first space provided. When you have finished matching, go back and fill in the second space to indicate whether the word part is a **root**, a **prefix**, or a **suffix**.

	Matching Number	Word Part	
a. magna	_____	_____	1. To build, form
b. dis-	_____	_____	2. To step
c. gress	_____	_____	3. Performs, serves to
d. de-	_____	_____	4. Large, powerful
e. struct	_____	_____	5. Apart or away, negative
f. –ive	_____	_____	6. Reverse, remove, reduce

"Summer Sun"

by Robert Louis Stevenson

Great is the sun, and wide he goes
Through empty heaven with repose;
And in the blue and glowing days
4   More thick than rain he showers his rays.

Though closer still the blinds we pull
To keep the shady parlour cool,
Yet he will find a chink or two
8   To slip his golden fingers through.

The dusty attic spider-clad
He, through the keyhole, maketh glad;
And through the broken edge of tiles
12   Into the laddered hay-loft smiles.

Meantime his golden face around
He bares to all the garden ground,
And sheds a warm and glittering look
16   Among the ivy's inmost nook.

Above the hills, along the blue,
Round the bright air with footing true,
To please the child, to paint the rose,
20   The gardener of the World, he goes.

TYPES OF WRITING

The two main genres, or types of writing, are **prose** and **poetry**. As you probably noticed, "Summer Sun" is quite different in style and content from "The Sun Chariot." However, the two pieces do share some similarities.

Use "Summer Sun" and "The Sun Chariot" to answer the following questions.

1. What is the genre of "Summer Sun"? _____

2. What is the genre of "The Sun Chariot"?_____
    Hint: It is sometimes considered the "opposite" of your answer for question 1.

3. After carefully reviewing both pieces of writing, explain in your own words the differences between the two genres or text styles that you identified in question 1. Remember, you are contrasting the style of the pieces, not the content!

    _____

    _____

    _____

    _____

    _____

    _____

4. Which of the following statements best represents a central theme that is shared by both "Summer Sun" and "The Sun Chariot"?

    A. Supernatural beings are responsible for the movement of the sun across the sky.

    B. Every day, the sun rises and moves across the sky, bringing light to the world.

    C. The light and heat provided by the sun are essential for life, but can also be destructive.

    D. Sunlight touches everything and everyone, and brings happiness wherever it goes.

5. A piece of writing often has more than one theme, or main idea. What is one theme you see in "Summer Sun" that is **not** found in "The Sun Chariot"? Be sure to use evidence from one or both pieces of writing to support your answer.

_____

_____

_____

_____

UNDERSTANDING FIGURATIVE LANGUAGE

Activity 1

Figurative language is not to be taken literally. Instead, it creates a **word picture** for the reader by using **symbols** and **comparisons** that help the reader "see" what the writer was "seeing" when he wrote the piece.

One of the most common forms of figurative language is **personification**, or the use of human qualities to describe or explain something nonhuman. By comparing the animal or object to a human, the writer makes his topic more understandable for the reader.

1. In "Summer Sun," Robert Louis Stevenson frequently uses the word "he." In the context of the poem, who or what is "he"? Which type of figurative language is being used in this case, and how do you know? Be sure to use evidence from the poem to support your answer.

_____

_____

_____

_____

2. In the second verse, the pronoun "we" is used. Is this an example of personification? Why or why not?

_____

_____

_____

3. In the third stanza of the poem, what object (besides the sun) is personified?

   A. The keyhole

   B. The tiles

   C. The attic

   D. The hay-loft

4. Explain the reason for your answer in question 3. Be sure to cite evidence from the poem that supports your claim.

   _____

   _____

   _____

   _____

Activity 2

Metaphors and **similes** are more types of figurative language that help the reader "see" an object or understand a concept by comparing it to something more familiar.

A **simile** uses the words *like* and *as* in the comparison. A **metaphor** compares things simply by stating that one "is" the other, or using the object of comparison as a replacement word for the subject that is being described.

1. Consider the phrase **golden fingers**, which appears in the second stanza. What type of figurative language is the phrase?

   _____

   What is being compared to **golden fingers**?

   _____

2. What **metaphor** for the sun appears in the fifth stanza?

   _____

   What do you think this metaphor means?

   _____

   _____

   _____

Standards L.6.4, L.6.5.a

The Reasons for the Seasons

1   One day, Hades, the god of the Underworld, happened to come up to Earth, and was wandering around on the island of Sicily. Little did he know that Aphrodite, the goddess of love, and her son, Cupid, noticed his arrival. Aphrodite had tried her tricks on most of the gods, but never on Hades, and was not about to pass up the perfect opportunity. She immediately called Cupid to her side.

2   "Look!" she said. "There is Hades! Quick, shoot him with one of your arrows, so that he falls in love. Then we will have some control in the Underworld, too!" Cupid did as he was told, and took aim. The arrow sailed through the air landed perfectly, piercing Hades' heart.

3   Just at that moment, Hades was passing by a field where Persephone, the daughter of the harvest goddess, Demeter, was picking some flowers. With Cupid's arrow stuck in his heart, he instantly fell in love with Persephone. Instead of **courting** her, though, he simply snatched her out of the field and into his chariot! Surprised and frightened, Persephone tried to call out to her mother and anyone else who might be in the area for help, but there was no answer.

4   As Hades sped toward the Underworld with Persephone captive in his chariot, a nymph named Cyane saw what was happening and came up out of a pool of water. "Stop!" she cried, "You shouldn't be doing this, Hades! You should have asked Demeter first, the mother of Persephone!"

5   But Hades was in no mood to argue with water nymphs. Instead of listening to Cyane, he threw down his royal staff so hard that a crack opened up in the Earth, taking him, his chariot, and Persephone straight down to the Underworld. Seeing that her advice had been ignored, and feeling very sorry for Persephone and her mother, Cyane began to sob, and cried so much that she turned into a stream of water.

6   Meanwhile, Demeter noticed that Persephone was missing, and was scouring the Earth for her. She searched day and night without resting, but could not find Persephone anywhere. Finally, she returned to Sicily, and came to the stream of water that had previously been Cyane. A piece of Persephone's clothing had been left behind there during the quick descent into the Underworld, and when Demeter recognized it, she knew that her daughter had been kidnapped.

7   Demeter wept, cursing heaven and earth for the loss of her daughter, until another water nymph, Arethusa, appeared before her. "Don't cry, Demeter," Arethusa said, "because I have been in the river that runs through the Underworld, and I have seen your daughter, Persephone! She is alive, and although she looks sad, she is the Queen of the Underworld, the wife of Hades!"

8   Demeter knew Persephone had been kidnapped, but she was still shocked to hear it confirmed, and extremely unhappy to hear that it was Hades who had done the kidnapping. She went immediately to Zeus, the ruler of all the gods, who was also Persephone's father.

9   "You must do something to get Persephone back from the Underworld!" she exclaimed. "Even if you will not act for my sake, at least think about your daughter! Consider, too, how dishonorable it is to have your own daughter carried away by the god of the Underworld!"

10 Zeus was not convinced by this argument. "It will not be dishonorable at all! After all, she is the wife of a god, and the Queen of the Underworld! Besides, Hades is my own brother. What could possibly be wrong with this marriage? However, since it seems to upset you so much, I will permit you to bring her back to Earth, as long as she has not eaten anything in the Underworld."

11 Demeter rushed immediately to the Underworld to claim her daughter, certain that Persephone would not have eaten anything during her stay. However, Persephone had not known that anyone who ate the food of the Underworld belonged to it forever, and had eaten seven pomegranate seeds while strolling through one of Hades' beautiful gardens. She was about to leave the Underworld with her mother when Ascalaphus, a spirit in charge of watching over the gardens, came forward.

12   "Stop!" he cried, pointing at Persephone. "You have eaten from the fruit trees of Hades, and now must stay in the Underworld forever!"

13   Persephone, angered by the spirit's interference, turned Ascalaphus into an owl, and Demeter was forced to return once more to the Earth without her daughter. Zeus, though, could tell how disappointed Demeter was. He also **ascertained** that the feud between Demeter and Hades over Persephone would never end if the situation continued as it was. He decided that a compromise was needed, and finally came up with a solution.

14   "Persephone," he said, "should continue to rule as Queen of the Underworld, the wife of my brother Hades. Six months out of the year, she should stay with him in the regions below. However, for the remaining six months, she should return to the Earth above, so that she can be with her mother, Demeter, and relieve her sadness."

15   Demeter accepted this agreement, and was finally able to be happy with her daughter by her side. Every year at the end of six months, though, Persephone must leave her mother and return to the Underworld. During those months, Demeter is sad, and without her joy, the warmth fades from the Earth and the crops are unable to grow, bringing autumn and winter to the land. The warmth and crops can only return when Persephone returns, bringing spring and summer to the Earth by bringing back Demeter's joy.

CENTRAL IDEAS, KEY DETAILS, AND SUMMARIES

Use "The Reasons for the Seasons" to answer the following questions.

Morals are usually **universal truths**, meaning that they apply to people throughout time and all over the world—not just the ancient Greeks!

1. What is the **theme** of the myth?

   _____

   _____

   _____

   _____

   _____

2. Identify a **moral**, or piece of advice about life, which appears in the myth. Support your answer with evidence from the text.

   _____

   _____

   _____

   _____

   _____

   _____

3. What can you **infer** about the goddess Aphrodite from the brief description provided in this myth? Support your answer with details from the text.

   _____

   _____

   _____

   _____

   _____

   _____

Standards RL.6.1, RL.6.2, RL.6.3

4. Which of the following statements **best** represents the relationship between Zeus and Demeter as it is portrayed in this myth?

   A. Demeter thinks that Zeus is a terrible father, but she goes along with what he says anyway because he is the most powerful god.

   B. Zeus does not always understand or agree with Demeter, but he tries to be considerate of her feelings and resolve her complaints.

   C. Demeter only has a good relationship with Zeus for the six months that Persephone is with her, and resents him for the rest of the year.

   D. Zeus tries to keep Demeter happy because he is worried that if he does not, she will make it winter all the time.

5. What is the **main problem** that moves the plot of the myth forward?

   A. Zeus disagrees with Demeter about the marriage of Hades and Persephone.

   B. Ascalaphus is turned into an owl because he speaks up about the pomegranate seeds.

   C. Cyane's efforts to stop the kidnapping of Persephone are ignored, leading to her death.

   D. Hades kidnaps Persephone and takes her to the Underworld without asking her mother.

UNDERSTANDING DENOTATIONS AND CONNOTATIONS

The **denotation** of a word is its definition as it would appear in a dictionary. **Connotation** refers to what a word makes people *think* and *feel*. It relates an idea, a concept, or an emotion that is being expressed. Authors use connotation to express thoughts and feelings more clearly. A connotation might be considered *positive* or *negative*. It may also be considered *stronger* or *weaker*.

Connotations create differences for the meaning of words. This is helpful when words with similar denotations are used. One way to think about this is as *shades of meaning*. To illustrate, an artist might use different tubes of paint that are all considered blue. One tube is pale blue, another is bright blue, while another is dark blue. If the artists asked you to pick a tube of blue paint, you could pick any of the three, but depending on what needs to be painted, one shade of blue would work better than the others.

Similarly, two or more words may have almost the same meaning when you look in the dictionary, but bring out different emotions in a reader because of the connotations (feelings or mental images) attached to each word.

In some cases, the connotations could be so strong that they are more important than the denotation.

Use "The Reasons for the Seasons" to answer the following questions.

1. Read these sentences taken from the text:

   *"Meanwhile, Demeter noticed that Persephone was missing, and was **scouring** the Earth for her. She **searched** day and night without resting, but could not find Persephone anywhere."*

   What connotations do **scouring** and **searched** present?

   _____

   _____

   _____

   Which word presents a **stronger** connotation? Explain your answer.
   Hint: It may help to think of the mental images that each word creates.

   _____

   _____

   _____

   _____

2. Read these sentences from the text:

   *"Demeter knew Persephone had been kidnapped, but she was still shocked to hear it confirmed, and extremely **unhappy** to hear that it was Hades who had done the kidnapping."*

   *"Zeus, though, could tell how **disappointed** Demeter was."*

   *"During those months Demeter is **sad**, and without her joy the warmth fades from the Earth and the crops are unable to grow, bringing autumn and winter to the land."*

   On another sheet of paper, swap the bolded words around to the other sentences.
   Do the sentences still make sense in the context of the myth? What does this indicate about the denotations of the words?

   _____

   _____

   _____

   _____

In the context of the story, which of the three words has a slightly different connotation? Support your answer using details from the text.

_____

_____

_____

_____

3. In this version of the myth, two different denotations of the word **cried** are used. Find an example of each denotation and write the sentences below:

_____

_____

_____

_____

4. Use a dictionary (print or online) to look up the word **cried**. Find two definitions that best fit each of your examples and record them in the space below:

_____

_____

_____

5. Read these sentences from the myth:

*"Surprised and frightened, Persephone tried to **call out** to her mother and anyone else who might be in the area for help, but there was no answer."*

*"You must do something to get Persephone back from the Underworld!" she **exclaimed**.*

Review your findings of the denotations for the word "cried" in questions 3 and 4. Which one is similar to the denotations for the highlighted words above?

_____

What different connotations do these three words with similar denotations have? Use evidence from the text to support your answer.

Hint: It will probably be helpful to consider the context in which they are used in the story.

Call out: _____

_____

Cry: _____

_____

Exclaim: _____

_____

WRITE YOUR EXPLANATION

After reading "The Sun Chariot" and "The Reasons for the Seasons," think critically about Greek and Roman myths. Use the graphic organizer to plan a short one-paragraph essay on the following subject:

Many Greek and Roman myths were created to provide explanations for natural events. However, in the modern world those explanations may seem unnecessary and outrageous. Why is the study of Greek and Roman mythology still important for students today, since modern science has disproved and replaced the explanations provided by many of the myths?

In your essay, you will need to explain why mythology is still an important subject for modern students. Before you begin, you may want to brainstorm a list of reasons on a separate piece of paper. If possible, use details from the myths you have read to support your reasons. Remember to use quotation marks if you quote directly from one of the myths.

Introduction (Topic sentence that states the main idea):

_____

_____

_____

Reason:

_____

_____

_____

_____

Reason:

_____

_____

_____

_____

Reason:

_____

_____

_____

_____

Explanation:

_____

_____

_____

_____

_____

_____

Explanation:

_____

_____

_____

_____

_____

_____

Explanation:

_____

_____

_____

_____

_____

_____

Conclusion (Concluding sentence that summarizes the main idea):

_____

_____

_____

REVIEW

Echo and Narcissus

1   One day, a water nymph named Liriope brought her newborn son to an old prophet named Tiresias. Like most mothers, she wanted to know whether her son would grow up into a strong man and live a long life. "If he never recognizes himself, he will," said Tiresias. Liriope and all the other people who heard the prophecy did not understand what Tiresias meant at the time, so they mostly ignored it. Sixteen years later, Liriope's son was nearly an adult, and known by all the people, men and women, as the beautiful Narcissus. But because he was so proud of his beauty, none of the compliments that he received from other people meant anything to him, and none of the young women were able to catch his eye. His beauty attracted the attention of a nymph named Echo, who fell in love with him the first time she saw him. However, she could not introduce herself because her voice had been taken away as a punishment by one of the gods. Instead, she could only communicate by repeating back the last words of any person who spoke to her.

2   One day, Narcissus accidentally wandered away from his companions and found himself alone in the woods. "Is anybody here?" he called out, hoping one of his companions would hear him.

3   "Here!" cried Echo, unable to do anything but repeat his words back to him. Narcissus was surprised to hear the voice, and looked all around, but the woods appeared to be **vacant**.

4   "Are you avoiding me?" he asked, not knowing who was speaking to him, or from what location. But Echo could only say the same thing back to him, rather than answer.

5   The conversation continued this way for some time, with Narcissus asking questions to the invisible nymph, and receiving only his own words in response. Finally, he started to lose patience and

said the one thing that he was certain would get a response: "Come here, so we can be together!"

6   This was the invitation that Echo had been waiting for! She abandoned her hiding place in the trees and **hastened** toward Narcissus, repeating "We can be together!" But when she reached him, he rushed away from her.

7   "Get your hands off of me!" he cried. "I will never be with you!" At that, he ran from the forest.

8   Echo, embarrassed that Narcissus had **spurned** her but still in love with him, never left the forest. She stayed there, in the woods and caves and between the mountains, until her body shriveled up and disappeared, and her bones turned to rocks. Only her voice could still be heard by the people who traveled to the lonely caves and mountains, as she repeated their words in the distance.

9   People saw what had happened to Echo, who had loved Narcissus and been cruelly rejected by him. They also saw that he continued to do the same to all those who declared their love for him, whether nymph or human. He was too vain to think that any of those who loved him were worthy of his affection. Finally, one person who felt the pain of Narcissus' dismissal prayed to the gods, "Please! Let Narcissus feel the same agony that he has caused to so many people! Let him fall in love with someone who does not return his regard!"

10   Nemesis, the goddess of vengeance, heard the prayer and resolved to answer it by leading Narcissus into a trap. One day, while he was out hunting in the forest, Narcissus decided to stop at a clear pool of water for a drink. The pool was so still that there was not a single ripple or wave in it, and when Narcissus leaned over to get a drink, he imagined that he saw a person staring back at him. He did not know that it was only his own reflection, and was immediately **smitten** by the face in the pool.

11   Narcissus tried to kiss the face he saw, to embrace it, to talk to it. "Why will you not come up out of that pool and be my beloved?" he cried. "My beauty has been **revered** by humans, and adored by the gods. How is it that I cannot win your love and persuade you to come up to me?" Of course, the face in the pool did not answer him, and Narcissus became as **forlorn** as all the hundreds of people who had once loved him. He refused to leave the pool for any reason, and instead sat by it without eating or drinking anything. When he would cry, and his tears would disturb the water so that his reflection disappeared even for a moment, he would panic, and beg the face to come back. Slowly, he began to get thin and weak, and his once beautiful appearance began to change. But it did not matter—he still loved the face in the water, and would not abandon it.

12   Echo saw what was happening to Narcissus, and although she was sad to see the one she had loved so dearly fall into such madness, she could also not forget how badly he had treated her. Still, every time he looked into the pool and sighed a sad "**Alas**!" at his silent reflection, the voice of Echo was audible in the distance: "Alas!" Finally, weakened because he refused to move from the pool, and heartbroken because his love was **unrequited,** Narcissus died. It was only then that the people remembered the words of old Tiresias, "If he never recognizes himself..." But it was too late. Narcissus would never be an old man, because he had seen his own face and fallen in love with it. Still, the gods mourned the death of such great beauty, and the nymphs prepared a funeral for him. Even Echo, mistreated as she had been, was sorry to see the young man go. But when she went with the other nymphs to the pool to retrieve Narcissus' body for the funeral, it was nowhere to be found. In its place was a beautiful flower, with small yellow petals in the center and larger white petals all around. They decided to call the flower Narcissus after the beautiful youth, and it has kept that name down to this very day.

Activity 1

Use "Echo and Narcissus" to complete the activity.

> **Unfamiliar Words:**
>
> vacant   spurned   hastened   smitten
> revered   forlorn   alas   unrequited

Using your favorite dictionary (either print or online), write a brief definition of each word in the space provided. If the word has more than one meaning, make sure you choose the one that is most appropriate for the context! Some of these definitions will help you in the questions that follow.

1. vacant: _____

2. spurn:_____

3. hasten: _____

4. smite (smitten): _____

5. revere: _____

6. forlorn:_____

7. alas: _____

8. unrequited:_____

9. Read this paragraph from the text:

"This was the invitation that Echo had been waiting for! She abandoned her hiding place in the trees and **hastened** *toward Narcissus, repeating 'We can be together!' But when she reached him, he rushed away from her. 'Get your hands off of me!' he cried. 'I will never be with you!' At that, he ran from the forest."*

Based on the definition for **hasten** that you found above and the context of the text, what other words in the paragraph have similar denotations? (*Hint:* There are two.)

_____

10. Read these sentences from the text:

"Echo, embarrassed that Narcissus had **spurned** *her but still in love with him, never left the forest."*

"People saw what had happened to Echo, who had loved Narcissus and been cruelly **rejected** *by him."*

"Finally, one person who felt the pain of Narcissus' **dismissal** *prayed to the gods."*

As the sentences demonstrate, **spurn**, **reject**, and **dismiss** have similar denotations. However, the words carry slightly different connotations. Using the context of the text, describe the connotations, or associations, that you have for each word that distinguished it from the other two. Support your answers, using evidence from the text when appropriate.

A. spurn _____

_____

_____

reject_____

_____

_____

dismiss _____

_____

_____

Activity 2

1. Read this sentence from the text:

    *"'Are you avoiding me?' he asked, not knowing who was speaking to him, or from what **location**."*

    Based on your knowledge of the word **location** and the context in the myth, the Latin root **"loc"** means:

    A. country

    B. distance

    C. side

    D. place

2. Read the two sentences from the text, paying special attention to the bolded words.

    *"The conversation continued this way for some time, with Narcissus asking questions to the **invisible** nymph, and receiving only his own words in response."*

    *"Still, every time he looked into the pool and sighed a sad 'Alas!' at his silent reflection, the voice of Echo was **audible** in the **distance**: 'Alas!'"*

    Based on your knowledge of the words and their context in the text, match the word parts to their definitions by writing the number of the correct answer in the space provided.

    A. vis _____   1. capable or

    B. ible _____   2. to hear

    C. dis _____   3. to see

    D. aud _____   4. not

    E. im _____   5. apart or away

UNDERSTAND

Let's apply the reading skills you covered in this section.

Activity 1

Use "Echo and Narcissus" to answer the following questions.

1. Is Narcissus a dynamic character or a static character? Explain your answer, using evidence from the text.

   _____

   _____

   _____

   _____

2. Which statement **best** describes the reason why Narcissus rejects Echo?
   A. Narcissus is annoyed at Echo because she hides from him and repeats everything he says.
   B. Narcissus wants to stay away from Echo because he knows her loss of speech was a punishment from the gods.
   C. Narcissus does not think that Echo deserves his love because he thinks too much of himself.
   D. Narcissus wants to see if Echo is really interested by running away and waiting for her to follow him.

3. What is one natural event that is explained by the text, and what is the explanation?

   _____

   _____

   _____

   _____

4. What **inference** can you draw about the flower, which appears at the end of the myth?

   _____

   _____

5. Which of the following is the main **problem** in the myth?

    A. Echo can only repeat what other people say.

    B. Narcissus is so vain that he treats people badly.

    C. Echo loves Narcissus even though he is mean to her.

    D. Narcissus is so beautiful that he cannot be around regular people.

6. How is the main problem of the myth solved? Write a brief summary of the **resolution**, or solution, to the problem below.

_____

_____

_____

_____

_____

7. Based on the information provided in the myth, could Narcissus' death have been avoided, even if he never gave up his vanity and became a better person? If so, how? Use evidence from the text to support your opinion.

_____

_____

_____

_____

_____

_____

8. Which of the following statements best represents the **theme** of the myth?

    A. Beauty can always be admired, but it is less valuable when kindness is missing.

    B. People should pay attention to prophecies, just in case they come true.

    C. Unrequited love is the worst kind of unhappiness a person can face.

    D. Revenge is most effective when it comes from someone with power.

DISCOVER

What would you say? Let's take what you have learned and write about it!

Write Your Narrative

Imagine that you are a person living in the distant past, like an ancient Greek or Roman. Without any modern scientific knowledge, you are very curious about the world and want to be able to explain why things happen in nature. You might believe in the supernatural, or you might not. What questions do you think you would have about the natural world?

Step 1: First, think about the folktales and myths that you have read in this book. What important "building blocks" did you notice in each piece of writing? If you said *Characters*, a *setting*, a *problem*, and a *solution*—you are correct. These are just a few of the key elements that can be found in many narratives.

Step 2: On a separate piece of paper, brainstorm questions about the natural world. They can be things that you understand but that would have been confusing to ancient people, or they can be things that you personally do not understand. Remember, when you are brainstorming there are no wrong ideas!

Step 3: Look at the results of your brainstorming session and think about each option. Determine which one you would like to use for your narrative.

Step 4: Now that you have picked your natural event, on that same piece of paper, write a brief summary of your "explanation". Was it the result of an argument? A natural disaster? Part of a love story? A complete accident? Is it funny? Sad? Neither? Try to keep your summary to one sentence. You can expand it later, but first you need an idea to expand on!

Step 5: What characters will you need for your story? Fill in the table below with your ideas. Some characters you think of may fall into more than one category, and you may not have any characters that fit into some categories. Remember, this is your story, so there are no wrong answers!

Main Characters	Side Characters	Human Characters
Good Characters	Bad Characters	Non-human Characters
Other		

Step 6: You have your characters, and you have a basic plot. Now it's time to get a little more detailed. Use the following template to outline your story. Then, decide whether the order makes sense, or whether you need to rearrange the events in your story. One of the most important parts of writing a narrative is making sure that it makes sense to the people who are reading it, and not just in your head! An outline can help make this happen.

Introduction: How will you start the narrative?

_____

_____

What is the problem in your story, or the question that needs to be answered? (This may or may not be the same as the natural event, depending on how your story is structured.)

_____

_____

What events will happen? These events may be in response to the problem or question, or may be part of solving the problem or question, or may just be events that are related in some way to the story as a whole. There are only three spaces for events here, but feel free to add as many as you need on a separate piece of paper! Be creative!

1. _____

2. _____

3. _____

How will the problem or question finally be solved, and how will the story end? Remember, if you have not already "explained" your natural event at this point, it will need to happen here!

_____

_____

Now you are ready to start writing your narrative! As you write, refer back to your outline. This will help you make sure that your story flows in a logical order. Remember to pay attention to spelling, punctuation, and grammar, especially if you are including dialogue in your story. When you are finished, have someone read your story and give you feedback. Once you have made any necessary changes, your narrative is complete!

Introduction (Set up your story):

_____

_____

_____

Event 1 (What first happened in your story? Use sensory details):

_____

_____

_____

_____

Event 2 (Then what happened? Use sensory details):

_____

_____

_____

_____

Event 3 (What finally happened? Use sensory details):

_____

_____

_____

_____

Conclusion (Describe the exciting moment):

_____

_____

_____

_____

Poetry

A poem is a piece of writing that can express an idea or an emotion, describe an object, or even tell a story. A poem can be about almost anything, and there are many different kinds of poetry. Some poems rhyme and have a rhythm; others do not. Poems can be as short as a few words or as long as an entire book. But since poems can be so different from each other, how can you tell if you are reading a poem and not prose, which is writing that is not poetry? In this Unit, you will practice reading poetry and identifying some of the things that make poetry special.

"Echoing Green"

William Blake (1789)

The sun does arise,
And make happy the skies.
The merry bells ring
To welcome the spring.
The skylark and thrush,
The birds of the bush,
Sing louder around,
To the bells' cheerful sound,
While our sports shall be seen
10   On the echoing green.

Old John with white hair
Does laugh away care,
Sitting under the oak,
Among the old folk.
They laugh at our play,
And soon they all say:
'Such, such were the joys
When we all, girls and boys,
In our youth-time were seen
20   On the echoing green.'

Till the little ones weary
No more can be merry;
The sun does descend,
And our sports have an end.
Round the laps of their mother
Many sisters and brothers,
Like birds in their nest,
Are ready for rest;
And sport no more seen
30   On the darkening green.

CENTRAL IDEAS, KEY DETAILS, AND SUMMARIES

Use "Echoing Green" to answer the following questions.

1. Provide a **summary** of the poem.

_____

_____

_____

_____

2. Which of the following is a **central idea** in "Echoing Green?" Circle the correct answer.
   A. Becoming old is part of life.
   B. Old folks do not understand the youth at play.
   C. Children become tired after long days in the park.
   D. The coming of spring is enjoyed by both people and the natural world.

3. Which details in the poem support your answer to question 2?

_____

_____

_____

_____

EXPAND YOUR KNOWLEDGE:
William Blake was not only a poet, but also a painter. In 1789, he wrote *Songs of Innocence*, a poetry collection written from a child's point of view. To read more about William Blake and his poetry, go to this link:
http://www.online-literature.com/blake/

W. BLAKE
1757-1827
MARILE ANIVERSĂRI CULTURALE 1957
40
BANI POSTA R.P. ROMÎNA

ANALYZING STRUCTURE

The organization of the stanzas in a poem contributes to the overall theme.

Example:

Little Lamb who made thee
Dost thou know who made thee
Gave thee life & bid thee feed.
By the stream & o'er the mead;
Gave thee clothing of delight,
Softest clothing wooly bright;
Gave thee such a tender voice,
Making all the vales rejoice!
Little Lamb who made thee
Dost thou know who made thee

Little Lamb I'll tell thee,
Little Lamb I'll tell thee!
He is called by thy name,
For he calls himself a Lamb:
He is meek & he is mild,
He became a little child:
I a child & thou a lamb,
We are called by his name.
Little Lamb God bless thee.
Little Lamb God bless thee.

The structure of these stanzas is **question and answer**. The first stanza asks a question, "Little Lamb, who made thee?" The last stanza attempts to answer that question. The stanzas contribute to the poem's overall theme—the child's question is profound yet simple because it touches upon the question that all people think about—where do we come from? What is the origin (nature) of life?

Use "Echoing Green" to answer the following question.

1. How does the organization of the stanzas contribute to the poem as a whole? What does it tell you about the poem's setting?

_____

_____

_____

_____

_____

_____

_____

WORD CHOICE AND TONE

The words and phrases authors choose to use in their texts also helps to set the tone or the mood. **Tone** is a feeling or attitude expressed by the words or phrases an author uses when writing. To set the tone, authors may sometimes use **rhythm** and **repetition**. **Rhythm** is regular, repeating patterns of sounds. Repetition happens when words are used again and again.

> **Example:** Karen and Hector climb up the **tree**,
> As they count to the number, **three**.
> Karen and Hector find a bird's **nest**.
> As they smile, they know, they won the **contest**.

Also, counting the number of **syllables** in each line of a stanza can help determine the author's tone. Syllables are ways to split words into parts or speech sounds.

> **Example:** Water has **2 syllables** (wa-ter)
> Word has **1 syllable**
> Available has **4 syllables** (a-vai-la-ble)

Use "Echoing Green" to answer the following questions.

1. Count the number of syllables in each line in the stanzas below.

Stanza 1

The sun does arise, _____

And make happy the skies. _____

The merry bells ring _____

To welcome the spring. _____

The skylark and thrush, _____

The birds of the bush, _____

Sing louder around, _____

To the bells' cheerful sound, _____

While our sports shall be seen _____

On the echoing green. _____

Stanza 3

Till the little ones weary _____

No more can be merry; _____

The sun does descend, _____

And our sports have an end. _____

Round the laps of their mother _____

Many sisters and brothers, _____

Like birds in their nest, _____

Are ready for rest; _____

And sport no more seen _____

On the darkening green. _____

2. How do the numbers of syllables in the lines in the first stanza compare to the third stanza? What kind of tone does each stanza create?

_____

_____

_____

_____

3. What's another way in which the author establishes rhythm in the poem? Provide an example.

_____

_____

_____

4. Describing birds in more than one place in the poem is an example of
   A. a simile
   B. rhythm
   C. repetition
   D. connotation

UNDERSTANDING FIGURATIVE LANGUAGE

Figurative Language: Sets of words or phrases that represent more than their literal, or actual, meaning. An example of figurative language includes similes.

Simile: Compares two unlike things using the words *like* or *as*.

> Example: Melody cleared her plate **as** a vacuum cleaner swallows dust.

Connotative Language: Ideas or feelings associated with a word, but are not part of that word's meaning. A word's connotation can be **positive** (good), **negative** (bad), or **neutral** (in the middle; not one way or the other).

> Example: The word, **dove**, has positive connotations because it is often associated with peace.

1. Does the poem have any similes? If so, provide one example on the lines below.

_____

_____

_____

2. Indicate whether each of the following phrases has a positive or negative connotation.
   A. Echoing green
   B. Darkening green
   C. The sun does arise
   D. Sitting under the oak tree
   E. The sun does descend

UNDERSTANDING PERSONIFICATION

Another way authors may choose to set the tone is by using **personification**. Personification is another example of figurative language. Personification gives a non-human object human qualities.

> Example: The stars danced playfully in the evening sky.

Use "Echoing Green" to answer the following questions.

1. Provide one example of personification from the poem.

   _____

   _____

2. How does the use of personification contribute to the overall **theme** of the poem?

   _____

   _____

"The Owl and the Pussycat"
Edward Lear (1871)

The Owl and the Pussy-Cat went to sea
In a beautiful pea-green boat:
They took some honey, and plenty of money
Wrapped up in a five-pound note.
The Owl looked up to the stars above,
And sang to a small guitar,
"O lovely Kitty, O Kitty, my love,
What a beautiful Kitty you are,
You are,
You are!
11   What a beautiful Kitty you are!"

Kitty said to the Owl,
"You elegant fowl,
How charmingly sweet you sing!
Oh! let us be married; too long we have tarried,
But what shall we do for a ring?"
They sailed away, for a year and a day,
To the land where the bong-tree grows;
And there in a wood a Piggy-wig stood,
With a ring at the end of his nose,
His nose,
His nose,
23   With a ring at the end of his nose.

"Dear Pig, are you willing to sell for one shilling
Your ring?" Said the Piggy, "I will."
So they took it away, and were married next day
By the turkey who lives on the hill.
They dined on mince and slices of quince,
Which they ate with a runcible spoon;
And hand in hand, on the edge of the sand,
They danced by the light of the moon,
The moon,
The moon,
34   They danced by the light of the moon.

"Owl and Pussycat" stamp; Great Britain, 1988.

ANALYZING STRUCTURE

Stanzas divide a poem so that it adds to the beauty, balance, and organization. It enables poets to shift moods, or to present different subject matters. This can affect the overall theme or message of a poem.

One type of stanza is the **ballad stanza.** A ballad stanza is a four-line stanza, which is known as a **quatrain**. Usually, only the second and fourth lines rhyme. The lines can be labeled in an a/b/c/b pattern because the second and fourth lines rhyme.

> **Example:** There lived a wife at Usher's Well, **(a)**
> And a wealthy wife was **she**; **(b)**
> She had three stout and stalwart sons, **(c)**
> And sent them over the **sea**. **(b)**

Activity 1

Use "The Owl and the Pussycat" to answer the following questions.

1. Even though each stanza in the poem has eleven lines, the poem uses a ballad stanza structure. Label the lines that indicate a ballad stanza. Write the letters next to each of the lines and refer to the example above for help.

> "Kitty said to the Owl,
> "You elegant fowl,
> How charmingly sweet you sing!
> Oh! let us be married; too long we have tarried,
> But what shall we do for a ring?"
> They sailed away, for a year and a day,
> To the land where the bong-tree grows;
> And there in a wood a Piggy-wig stood,
> With a ring at the end of his nose,
> His nose,
> His nose,
> With a ring at the end of his nose."

2. What important action takes place in this stanza? _____

3. How does this stanza contribute to the overall theme and organization of the poem?

_____

Activity 2

A poet may also use a refrain throughout a poem to emphasize, or stress, certain ideas in the poem.

Refrain: A line, phrase, or group of lines repeated at different points throughout a poem, usually at the end of each stanza.

> Example: The woods are lovely, dark, and deep,
> But I have promises to keep,
> And miles to go before I sleep,
> And miles to go before I sleep.
>
> (Excerpt from "Stopping By Woods on a Snowy Evening," by Robert Frost)

Use "The Owl and the Pussycat" to answer the following questions.

1. Write the **refrain** from each of the stanzas below.

    Stanza 1: _____

    _____

    _____

    Stanza 2: _____

    _____

    _____

    Stanza 3: _____

    _____

    _____

2. How do the refrains contribute to the tone of the poem as a whole, and the overall message of the poem?

    _____

    _____

    _____

COMPARING MEDIA

The experience of reading a story or a poem can be very different from listening to it or watching a video or a live performance. For example, a reader might miss some important details when reading a poem, but might catch those same details when listening to the poem being read aloud.

Visit the following website to watch a video of "The Owl and the Pussycat."
www.watchknowlearn.org/Video.aspx?VideoID=33800&CategoryID=9474

Answer the following questions after you have watched the video.

1. Describe the pace at which the narrator in the video recites, or says, the poem.

   _____

   _____

2. Based on the video, what is the tone and mood of the poem?

   _____

   _____

3. How does seeing the characters in the video affect the poem as a whole?

   _____

   _____

   _____

4. Which experience do you prefer, and why?

   _____

   _____

   _____

5. Describe anything you noticed in the video that you missed when reading the poem.

   _____

   _____

   _____

WRITE YOUR ARGUMENT

An argumentative essay is an essay that requires you to research a topic and then pick a position on the topic. Your position should be supported by different pieces of credible evidence.

Students listening to a village orchestra and choir, c.1800s.

Write an argumentative essay on the following question:

While some poets choose to write their poems in ballad stanzas, others write their poems in couplets (two lines that appear one after the other; the last word or phrase of the lines rhyme). Which of the two—ballad stanzas or couplets—were more popular during the 1800s?

Step 1: Introduce the topic clearly and provide a preview of what will follow.

Step 2: Develop the topic clearly and use relevant details to back up your thoughts and ideas.

Step 3: You may include diagrams, charts, or tables if you choose.

Step 4: Use facts and concrete details, and make sure you cite your sources.

Step 5: Use a formal and objective tone, be consistent in your verb tenses, and use different transitions to make your writing more interesting.

Step 6: Provide a concluding statement that brings everything together and supports your explanation.

Use the following chart to help brainstorm ideas for your essay.

Introduction: _____

_____

_____

Topic Sentence 1: _____

_____

_____

_____

Topic Sentence 2: _____

_____

_____

_____

Topic Sentence 3: _____

_____

_____

_____

Conclusion: _____

_____

_____

REVIEW

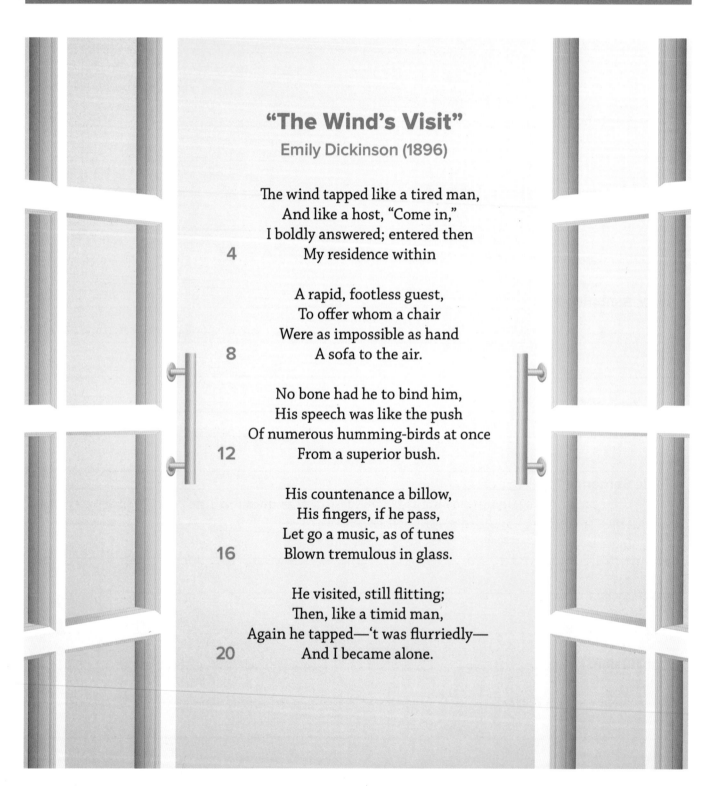

"The Wind's Visit"

Emily Dickinson (1896)

The wind tapped like a tired man,
And like a host, "Come in,"
I boldly answered; entered then
4   My residence within

A rapid, footless guest,
To offer whom a chair
Were as impossible as hand
8   A sofa to the air.

No bone had he to bind him,
His speech was like the push
Of numerous humming-birds at once
12   From a superior bush.

His countenance a billow,
His fingers, if he pass,
Let go a music, as of tunes
16   Blown tremulous in glass.

He visited, still flitting;
Then, like a timid man,
Again he tapped—'t was flurriedly—
20   And I became alone.

Activity 1

Use "The Wind's Visit" to answer the following questions.

1. In the poem, "The Wind's Visit," Dickinson uses figurative language to bring the characters to life. Identify two types of figurative language used in the poem and define each type.

    _____

    _____

    _____

    _____

    _____

    _____

2. Provide an example of each type of figurative language listed above from the poem.

    _____

    _____

    _____

    _____

    _____

    _____

3. How does each type of figurative language you identified in question 1 help the author to express the theme of the poem and add meaning to the poem?

    _____

    _____

    _____

    _____

    _____

    _____

4. Provide your own examples of each of the figurative languages listed above.

_____

_____

_____

_____

_____

5. Based on the descriptions of the wind in the poem, which of the following does the wind most likely resemble?

A. a friend

B. a ghost

C. a stranger

D. an intruder

Challenge: Write a three-stanza ballad poem about an animal. Make sure you use the figurative language you learned about in previous units.

_____

_____

_____

_____

_____

_____

_____

_____

_____

UNDERSTAND

Activity 1

Use "The Wind's Visit" to answer the following questions.

1. **Summarize** the poem in your own words.

_____

_____

_____

_____

_____

2. What is the **theme** of the poem?

_____

_____

_____

_____

3. Which details in the poem support your answer to question 3?

_____

_____

_____

4. What can you **infer** from the poem?
    A. The narrator prefers to be alone.
    B. The narrator is confused by the visitor.
    C. The narrator feels bothered by the wind.
    D. The narrator appreciates the wind's presence.

Activity 2

1. How did the narrator feel about the visit from the wind? Circle the correct answer.

    A. She welcomed it, and felt lonely when the wind left.

    B. She wanted the visit, and begged for the visitor to stay longer.

    C. She dreaded the visit, and was glad to be alone when the wind left.

    D. She felt miserable during the visit, but felt lonely when the visit ended.

2. Who is the narrator in the poem? How can you tell?

    _____

    _____

    _____

3. Does the narrator's description of the visitor change from the beginning to the end of the poem? Which evidence from the poem supports your answer?

    _____

    _____

    _____

    _____

Activity 3

1. How does the description of the wind in the second stanza contribute to the poem's overall **theme**?

    _____

    _____

    _____

    _____

2. Which of the following is a correct description of the poem?

    A. It uses couplets.

    B. It has no rhyme.

    C. It has three stanzas.

    D. It uses ballad stanzas.

Standards RL.6.2, RL.6.3, RL.6.5

3. Label the **rhyme pattern** in the following quatrain from the poem.

His countenance a billow,   _____

His fingers, if he pass,   _____

Let go a music, as of tunes   _____

Blown tremulous in glass.   _____

4. Is this rhyme pattern the same throughout the poem? Explain your answer.

_____

_____

_____

_____

_____

5. How does the repetition of the word **tapped** in the first and last stanzas contribute to the poem's theme?

_____

_____

_____

_____

_____

Digging Deeper

Sometimes, the way we read a poem out loud is different from the way others read it, or how the author intended for the poem to be read. To hear "The Wind's Visit" read out loud, go to this link: *http://etc.usf.edu/lit2go/115/the-poems-of-emily-dickinson- series-two/4467/nature-poem-30-the-winds-visit/*

DISCOVER

What would you say? Let's take what you have learned and write about it!

Write Your Narrative

Throughout the previous units, you have learned about different types of narratives, including poems and short, fictional stories. You have also learned that authors of narrative texts use different tools to express their ideas! They may use figurative language, such as similes and personification, dialogue between characters, lots of details, rhyme patterns, or even repetition to make sure that readers understand what is being said in the narrative. Now, it is your turn to write a narrative! Imagine that you are a poet or author of a short story. Write a poem or story about a time when you felt lonely. Your story or poem can be based on a real-life experience, or it can be fictional!

Gathering Information

Step 1: Reread the poems in Unit 9.

Step 2: Ask an adult to help you search on the Internet for more information on writing a poem or a short story.

Hint: A good search engine to use is *www.google.com*, and you might use the phrases "how to write a good short story" or "what makes a good poem" in your initial search.

Step 3: Read the articles you locate and take some notes on the information you discover.

Hint: If you know the names of any famous poets or authors, you may want to do a search on their work to help you gather your thoughts and to brainstorm some ideas. Here are some names of poets and authors you may want to start with:
1. Robert Frost
2. Shel Silberstein
3. Edgar Allen Poe
4. Gwendolyn Brooks

Step 4: Fill out the story web, on the next page, noting the different components, or parts, of a good narrative.

PLOT

CHARACTERS   SETTING

TITLE

CONFLICT   RESOLUTION

Starting to Write

Step 5:   Use the graphic organizer to arrange the details that you put in your story web. Set the scene by providing information the reader will need to understand your story or poem.

Who is in the story?

_____

_____

_____

Share your emotions, feelings, reactions:

_____

_____

Sensory details:

_____

_____

Catch the reader's attention with your title and first sentence: _____

_____

(Beginning) First:_____

_____

(Detail) Next: _____

_____

(Detail) Then: _____

_____

(Detail) Last: _____

_____

Conclusion:_____

Step 6: Take the information from your graphic organizer and write your narrative in complete sentences if you are writing a short story, or in stanzas if you are writing a poem. Be sure to include transition words and phrases to link your ideas.

Transition Words and Phrases You Might Choose To Use

| for instance | also | in fact | for example | first | although |
| for this reason | in addition | however | therefore | finally | next |

*Remember to use a comma after transition words that begin sentences!

Also, remember to use figurative and connotative language, as well as dialogues between characters to make your narrative more interesting. Make sure that your story or poem flows in a natural, logical way that makes sense to the reader.

Step 7: Ask an adult to read what you have written. Work together to do the following:

- Make sure you have introduced a narrator and characters, and established a clear setting and introduction.

- Check to make sure you have expressed the mood and tone that you want the readers to feel.

- Because this is a narrative, you can use "I" and "you" in your story or poem.

- Look for places where you can make better word choices. Choose a few words from your essay and consult a thesaurus to see if you can choose better words to use.

- Proofread your narrative for errors in grammar and mechanics.

- Provide a concluding statement that brings everything together and supports the events that happen throughout the story.

- Make sure your narrative creates a clear picture for the reader from the beginning to the end of the story.

Answer Key

Reading and Writing: Informational Texts

Unit 1—Wonders of the World

Lesson 1—The Great Wall of China

Page 14. Central Ideas, Key Details, and Summaries: 1. C; 2. Answers will vary. Sample response: The Great Wall of China is a modern wonder of the world because of its history, enormous size, and the fact that it was created solely by human labor without the use of heavy machinery; 3. Answers will vary. Sample response: "The building of this incredible wall began under Emperor Qin, China's very first emperor, who ruled over 2,000 years ago," and "While part of the Great Wall was built under the rule of Emperor Qin, most of what we see today was built under the Ming Dynasty, a series of emperors from the Ming family that ruled China from 1368 to 1644"; 4. Answers will vary. Sample response: Emperor Qin started the work on the wall so it is important to discuss him before the Ming Dynasty.

Page 15. Understanding Vocabulary: 1. Submit is a verb that means to accept or yield to a superior force or to the authority or will of another person; 2. The Ming Dynasty was a series of emperors from the Ming family that ruled China from 1368 to 1644; Spelling Correctly: 1. structure; 2. elevations; 3. accomplishment; 4. caution; 5. wondrous

Lesson 2—Stonehenge

Page 18. Central Ideas, Key Details, and Summaries: 1. Answers will vary. Possible response: Stonehenge is an ancient monument that was built in three phases over a 1,500 year period of time. Archaeologists are not sure who built Stonehenge or why, but there are many theories about it; 2. Answers will vary. Possible responses: There are many theories about who built Stonehenge, but current archaeologists believe "that several different tribes of people helped to build Stonehenge over a period of 1,500 years"; Archaeologists don't know why Stonehenge was built, but some theories are "that it was a religious place of worship, a burial ground, or an astronomical observatory"; 3. Answers will vary. Possible response: The author states that several hundred years after the first stage of building, "80 bluestones were placed in a horseshoe shape at the center of the bank." That means there was a second stage of building.

Page 19. Analyzing Structure: 1. The author used headings and captions on illustrations; 2. Answers will vary. Possible response: The headings help separate the important ideas the author discussed, and the captions help readers to make connections between information in the text and the photos; 3. Answers will vary. Possible response: The author uses a chronological method for developing the ideas in the second paragraph. He or she tells what happened first, second, and third; Understanding Vocabulary: 1. Monument is a noun that means a building or place that is important because of when it was built or because of something in history that happened there; 2. Archaeologist is a noun that means a scientist who studies material remains (such as fossil relics, artifacts, and monuments) of past human life and activities.

Unit 2—Celebrations of the World

Lesson 1—Chinese New Year

Page 23. Central Ideas, Key Details, and Summaries: 1. C; 2. Answers will vary. Sample response: Three traditions associated with Chinese New Years are cleaning the house "to sweep away all the bad luck of the previous year," having a family dinner where jiaozi dumplings are served, and giving gifts called hong bao.

Page 24. 3. Answers will vary. Sample responses: Children enjoy Chinese New Year celebrations because they get a whole month off from school; children enjoy Chinese New Year celebrations because they receive red envelopes containing money or sweets; 4. Answers will vary. Possible response: In the legend of the *Nian*, the only things that would scare it away were loud noises and bright lights. Modern Chinese New Year celebrations still have loud noises and bright lights in the form of firecrackers and fireworks. The *Nian* was also supposed to be scared away by the color red, and red is still one of the main colors used in Chinese New Year celebrations.

Page 25. Reflexive and Intensive Pronouns: 1. ourselves (I); 2. himself (R); 3. herself (I); 4. themselves (I); 5. herself (R); 6. himself (I); 7. themselves (I); 8. myself (I)

Page 27. Active Voice and Passive Voice: Answers will vary but should be similar to the following: In early China, *Nian*, a furious mountain beast, attacked villages every month. A wise old man in the village made a suggestion to conquer the monster. The villagers beat drums, wore red robes, and threw firecrackers to frighten the beast. These loud noises and bright lights scared away the *Nian* for a year. Modern Chinese people perform the traditional lion dance every year in New Year celebrations to honor the Chinese legend.

Lesson 2—Carnival in Rio de Janeiro

Page 29. Central Ideas, Key Details, and Summaries: 1. C; 2. Answers will vary. Possible responses: Many traditions of the past are included in modern day celebrations. In the 1800s the rich, working class, and poor people held parades where they wore costumes and masks and danced in the streets. African Samba music and dance had a big effect on Carnival. Today, top Samba schools compete for the championship during the last two days of the Carnival.

Page 30. 3. Answers will vary. Possible responses: In 2011 4.9 million people attended Carnival. The *Guiness Book of World Records* recorded it as the largest celebration in the world; 4. Answers will vary. Possible responses: African tradition has a major influence over modern-day Carnival celebrations because the samba music, which is the basis of the samba dancing, was largely based on African music; African slaves had a large influence on the culture of Brazil. Samba, the type of music that is played during Carnival, comes from a blend of African slave songs and Brazilian street music.

Page 31. Pronoun Cases: 1. P; 2. O; 3. S; 4. P; 5. O

Page 32. The Case of "I" and "Me": 1. me; 2. I; 3. me; 4. I; 5. I

Unit 3—Ancient Civilizations of the World

Lesson 1—Fall of the Mayan Empire

Page 37. Central Ideas, Key Details, and Summaries: 1. A; Determining Point of View and Purpose: 1. C; 2. B

Page 38. Analyzing Structure: 1. The author used headings, captions on illustrations, and a list; 2. Answers will vary. Possible response: The list was most helpful to me because it helped me keep the theories straight as I read about them; 3. Answers will vary. Possible response: The second paragraph provides background information on the Maya civilization to illustrate how great it once was; 4. Answers will vary. Possible response: The first sentence in the conclusion is important because this is where the author states his or her opinion on what brought about the collapse of the Mayan Empire; Evaluating an Argument: 1. Answers will vary. Possible response: The author claims that it is a combination of the expert theories that brought about the collapse of the Mayan Empire; 2. D

Page 39. Understanding Vocabulary: 1. Answers will vary. Possible response: The author claims that it is a combination of the expert theories that brought about the collapse of

the Mayan Empire; 2. D; Analogies: 1. words; 2. stone; 3. collapse; 4. thumb

Lesson 2—Decline of the Egyptian Empire

Page 43. Central Ideas, Key Details, and Summaries: 1. Answers will vary. Possible response: The Egyptian Empire was once a very powerful empire that lasted over three thousand years but declined due to several factors including economic issues, military issues, and religious issues; Determining Point of View and Purpose: 1. The author's purpose was to inform and teach; 2. D

Page 44. Evaluating an Argument: 1. Answers will vary. Possible response: The author claims no single factor can be blamed for the fall of the Egyptian Empire but that several factors combined to cause the collapse; 2. Answers will vary. Possible response: Economic, military, and religious issues were probably factors in the decline of the Egyptian Empire; 3. C

Page 45. Understanding Vocabulary: 1. Reversed is a verb that means the past tense of to move backward; 2. Decline is a verb that means to become smaller, fewer, or less; decrease; Analogies: 1. pharaoh; 2. conquer; 3. wealthy

Stop and Think! Units 1–3 Review

Page 49. Activity 1: Answers will vary. Possible response: The culture of the Roman Empire has a great influence on our lives today, even though we don't think about it much. For instance, Romans invented socks (called soccus) and shoes as we know them. Some even say they invented cosmetics such as lipstick. Romans also invented some very ornate jewelry, and used rings a lot. They used these rings for showing friendship and engagements and also at weddings; Activity 2: 1. Solution is a noun that means a method of solving a problem; 2. Previously is an adjective that means earlier in time or order, before; 3. Barbarians is a noun that means (in ancient times) members of a community or tribe not belonging to one of the great civilizations.

Stop and Think! Units 1–3 Understand

Page 50. Activity 1: 1. A; 2. Answers will vary. Possible response: The author uses examples involving language and government to show the influence of the Roman Empire on our modern-day life. The author mentions that our alphabet and many root words in the English language come from the Romans and that the Romans "had a constitution, written laws, and branches of government." This is just like the current government of the United States; 3. Answers will vary. Possible response: The author explains that the size of the Roman Empire contributed to its collapse because it grew too large to govern, required a large army to keep control, and that "Romans themselves did not want to serve in the army."

Answer Key

Unit 4—Biomes of the World
Lesson 1—Siberian Tundra

Page 57. Determining Point of View and Purpose: 1. D; 2. C; 3. Answers will vary. Possible response: Yes, the author clearly expresses her point of view. She provides evidence that shows that the melting permafrost could destroy the habitat and human environment in the Siberian tundra. She talks about the crater, which was created by methane gas and explains that if the permafrost continues to melt, buildings, soil, and communities will be destroyed.

Page 58. Understanding Figurative Language: 1. C; 2. The metaphor "the ground is a muddy soup" compares the swampy ground to soup because it is so wet and mushy.

Page 59. 1. Global warming has a negative connotation; 2. Ecosystem has a neutral connotation; 3. Communities have a positive connotation; 4. Summer has a positive connotation; 5. Stalagmites and stalactites have a neutral connotation.

Page 60. Using Pronouns Correctly: 1. Vague pronouns. It is not clear what the word, This, at the beginning of the second sentence refers to; 2. Answers may vary but should make the vague pronoun clearer. Possible response: Researchers worry that recent findings, along with the discovery of two new craters in Siberia, indicate that there will be changes to the Siberian climate as well as its local habitats and environments. These changes could mean fallen buildings, eroded soil (worn away), destroyed ecosystems, and distressed communities; 3. When the ice and snow melt, they consequently form puddles called thermokarsts; therefore, the summers in the tundra are also marshy, a term which means that the ground is wet and muddy!

Page 61. 1. A. 2; B. 3; C. 1; 2. Most researchers themselves agree that daily human activities such as driving or producing electricity also create extra amounts of carbon dioxide, methane, and other greenhouse gases in the atmosphere, trapping heat and creating a warming effect.

Page 62. Understanding Vocabulary: 1. D; 2. Answers may vary: Possible answer: Remained in the dark in the sentence, "Yet, scientists have remained in the dark about the release of greenhouse gases from melting permafrost" means that the scientists still don't have a lot of information about how the greenhouse gases are being released from the melting permafrost.

Page 63. Cause and Effect Relationships: 1. The two underlined words show a cause/effect relationship; 2. Explanations may vary. Possible response: When is a time word that signals the action of something happening; in this case, ice and snow melting. Consequently is a result of the action happening. The reader learns that puddles are a result of ice and snow melting because of the two signal

words, when and consequently; Challenge: 1. Answers will vary. Possible response: Due to winds that travel between 30 and 60 miles per hour, bare skin can become frozen in about thirty seconds; 2. Answers will vary. Possible response: Because roads, railways, power lines, and businesses are all built on permafrost, scientists in the area note that the melting of the permafrost could damage the infrastructure of the communities in the Siberian tundra.

Lesson 2—The Wonder of the Amazon

Page 68. Understanding Figurative Language: 1. The "Heart of the Amazon" is a metaphor because the author is comparing Manaus to a human body part—a heart. When you compare two things that are different without using the words *as* or *like*, you are using a metaphor; 2. "Heart of the Amazon" means that Manaus is at the center of Amazon; its location is centralized.

Page 69. Combining Ideas: 1. The rainy season in Manaus is from December to May. According to the table, it rains the most in March and the least in August.

Page 70. 2. Between medium and low should be marked; 3. The under canopy receives a little more sunlight than the shrubs, but a little less sunlight than the canopy.

Page 71. Using Punctuation Correctly: 1. Rainfall and high humidity contribute to the growth of the different types of vegetation (groups of plants, bushes, grass, and trees); 2. If people continue to cut down the trees and clear the land for other uses (a process called deforestation), the carbon will be released into the air and contribute to global warming; 3. The WWF organization (represented in 100 countries) is connecting with local governments in Brazil to secure land in the Amazon to prevent deforestation.

Page 73. Credible Sources: 1. The "Siberian Tundra" source is most credible because the information in that article comes from a journal, which is a trustworthy source. The information in "Amazon Rainforest" comes from someone's website, so it may not be as credible.

Unit 5—Nature's Effect on the World
Lesson 1—The Lost City of Pompeii

Page 77. Central Ideas, Key Details, and Summaries: 1. B; 2. Answers will vary. Possible response: The author introduces and analyzes the central idea in the text by describing how beautiful and thriving Pompeii was before the volcanic eruption. For the rest of the passage, the author focuses on how Mount Vesuvius erupted and the outcome of the eruption, as well as the aftermath to show how the eruption changed Pompeii; 3. Answers will vary. Possible response: Pompeii was a busy and beautiful city that many people visited. However, it was located at the bottom of a volcano,

Mount Vesuvius. In 79 C.E. Vesuvius erupted and the city of Pompeii was covered in the dust and ash from the explosion. The city was buried so quickly that it was preserved, and explorers have been able to uncover it and learn about life in Pompeii before the eruption. Scientists continue to study Mount Vesuvius to learn more about the eruption that buried Pompeii, and to possibly find out when Mount Vesuvius will erupt next.

Page 78. Making Words: 1. Dynamic–powerful; Amphitheater–a round theater, where people can see from both sides; Abnormal–away from the normal; Extraterrestrial–outside or beyond Earth; Action–the state of doing; 2. Answers will vary.

Page 79. Understanding Vocabulary: 1. Erupt means to explode violently all of a sudden; 2. C; 3. A; 4. Answers will vary. Possible response: Preservative in this sentence means something that saves and protects something else from being ruined.

Lesson 2–Tsunamis—Waves Without Borders

Page 82. Central Ideas, Key Details, and Summaries: 1. C; 2. Homes and communities in Minamisanriku, Japan were destroyed in the tsunami in 2011; A tsunami struck the island of Crete. Historians believe that this disaster is what led to the downfall of the Minoans; 3. Predictions of the disasters were faulty; the actual events were much worse than predicted. Leaders must work hard to be sure that such mistaken predictions never happen again; 4. Answers will vary. Possible response: Earthquakes and tsunamis are powerful natural disasters that can have lasting and damaging effects. Countless numbers of homes, communities, people, and entire civilizations have been changed forever because of these events. Today, people are spreading the word and giving warning information so that other people can be prepared.

Page 83. Spelling Correctly: 1. absolutely; 2. bulletin; 3. distinguish; 4. tales, fables

Page 84. Maintaining Style and Proper Tone: 1. Begun should be replaced with began; 2. Are should be replaced with were; 3. Share should be replaced with shared; Understanding Vocabulary: 1. Magnitude–size; 2. Optimistic–care-free, seeing the bright side of things

Page 85. 3. Predicted–to have said that something will or might happen in the future; 4. Hurl–to throw something with force

Page 86. Using Evidence and Sources: 1. B; 2. Answers will vary. Possible response: A news article is the most credible source listed in the options; this means that it provides trustworthy information that can be used and cited in a research paper; 3. B; 4. Answers may vary. The president

of the PTA at JFK's School is not an expert in natural disasters. Any information that he provides may or may not be accurate; 5. Explanations will vary. Possible response: I would use the natural disaster survivor I found online. When I conduct my own interview, I am providing first-hand information that the teacher wants.

Page 87. Write in Your Own Words: For questions 1-3, answers will vary. Possible answers: 1. Even though we do not have records of every tsunami that has occurred, for thousands of years, tsunamis have been happening in different parts of the world; 2. According to researchers, the Minoan civilization fell because a tsunami hit the Island of Crete thousands of years ago.

Page 88. 3. People have a difficult time going back to the way life was before a tsunami or earthquake occurred because of the negative results from the disaster.

Unit 6–Animals and People of the World
Lesson 1–Australia's Lightweight Champions

Page 95. Central Ideas, Key Details, and Summaries: 1. C; 2. To introduce the idea that kangaroos have strong legs and tails, the author states that a kangaroo can jump as much as thirty feet in one hop and travel at more than forty miles per hour, which is faster than what a car travels in a school zone. In the second paragraph, the author discusses the fact that kangaroos belong to the "Macropodidae" group, which means big foot. In the third and fourth paragraphs, the author describes how kangaroos use their hind legs and tails to fight their predators, and use their forelegs to box each other during mating seasons. In the final paragraph, the author explains new research findings showing that a kangaroo's tail is like a "fifth leg"; 3. Answers will vary. Possible response: Kangaroos are well-known as Australian marsupials. They are unique animals with many interesting features, but especially their large feet and strong tails. Kangaroos use their feet and tail to defend themselves against predators and to box with other kangaroos to prove superiority. The tail is so strong that it is almost like a fifth leg the kangaroo can use when it moves.

Page 96. Using Punctuation Correctly: 1. A; Challenge: 1. Answers may vary. Possible response: Most people, however, may not know that kangaroos can stand at around six feet tall, making them the tallest of all marsupials—a class of animals that carry their young in a pouch. 2. Answers may vary. Possible response: Shortly after they leave the comfort of their mothers' pouches, joeys learn that they have a few predators (including humans and dingoes, or wild dogs), and must learn how to protect themselves.

Lesson 2—Saving the Mountain Gorilla

Page 100. Combining Ideas: 1. When mountain gorillas first leave the band, they are in the blackback stage of their lives, when they are between eight and twelve years old; 2. The silverback usually becomes the leader of the group around age twelve or older, according to the information in the table; 3. The Virunga Mountains are located in the North/Northwest area of Rwanda and serves as a border between that country and three other countries, Uganda, Tanzania, and the Democratic Republic of Congo; 4. The Virunga Mountains are about 2000 meters above sea level; 5. Volcanoes National Park is located between Rwanda and Uganda.

Page 101. Hyperbole: 1. A

Page 102. Denotations and Connotations: 2. A. Shelter: A place or structure that gives protection against weather or danger. Home: The place where a person or animal lives; 2. B. Connotations will vary. Possible response: A place or territory that belongs to the gorillas where humans should not be; 3. A. Youthful: Young in actuality or appearance; Childish: Typical of or fit for a child; 3. B. The second sentence, which uses "childish"; 3. C. Positive; 3. D. Connotations may vary. Possible response: Youthful has the connotation of being young, healthy, and happy no matter someone's actual age.

Lesson 3—Making Friends with Mountain Gorillas—Following the Footsteps of Dian Fossey

Page 106. Different Ways to Express the Same Idea: 1. Answers may vary. Possible answer: In "Saving the Mountain Gorilla," the author is trying to inform the reader about mountain gorillas and some of the hardships they face, including being hunted and having their habitats destroyed. The author believes mountain gorillas should be protected. In "Making Friends with Mountain Gorillas," the scientist being interviewed has been working with mountain gorillas for a long time and seems to have information about the species that others do not have. She uses personal stories rather than research to support her claims. The scientist is also in favor of protecting this endangered species; 2. Answers may vary. Possible answer: The scientist loves mountain gorillas and feels more should be done to ensure their safety in their habitats; 3. Answers may vary. Possible answer: Even though one author has more personal experience than the other, both have a similar purpose, to inform the reader about an ongoing issue; Challenge: Answers will vary. Possible answer: The scientist's personal experiences with the gorillas make the information seem very trustworthy. It also makes gorillas sound less like wild animals and more like friends. Both authors love the gorillas and want to motivate the reader to help protect them, but

the scientist who has actually lived with the gorillas seems to feel more strongly about the gorillas.

Lesson 4—Wangari' Maathai—A Lady Like No Other

Page 110. Central Ideas, Key Details, and Summaries: 1. B; 2. C; 3. Answers will vary. Possible answer: Wangari' Maathai dedicated her life to helping her home country of Kenya restore its forests. She created the Green Belt Movement, which employed over 30,000 people and had given jobs to physically disabled people and those living in rural areas who otherwise would not have been able to work. Her work led to the Pan American Green Belt Movement, where other African countries follow the same method of replanting trees to stop deforestation as in Kenya.

Page 111. Determining Point of View and Purpose: 1. D; 2. Answers will vary. Possible answers: Wangari' Maathai spent most of her life showing others the importance of taking care of the earth. She started the Green Belt Movement as a way to help her country and create opportunities for women and young people. She became a political and environmental activist to help her country as well as women and achieved a great deal in her lifetime; Evaluating an Argument: 1. C; 2. C

Page 112. 3. D; Reflexive and Intensive Pronouns: 1. ourselves, (I); 2. herself, (R)

Page 113. 3. herself, (I); 4. myself, (I); 5. themselves, (R)

Stop and Think! Units 4–6 Review

Page 117. Activity 1: 1. Answers will vary. Possible response: There are more geysers here (in the United States at Yellowstone National Park) than there are anywhere else in the world; 2. Answers will vary. Possible response: Cone geysers, such as the Riverside Geyser, erupt from a stream of water in a narrow cone; Activity 2: 1. Answers will vary. Possible response: Because the water cannot flow freely to the surface, there is a lot of pressure, and the water cannot boil. The pressure causes steam to form when the water is rising; 2. The combination of the overflowing river and boulders was extremely powerful, and together, they destroyed much of what they found in their path; 3. On October 4, 1981, for instance, a typhoon caused a local river, the Gersenaya, to flood; the flood pushed heavy rocks and boulders downstream.

Stop and Think! Units 4–6 Understand

Page 118. Activity 1: 1. B; 2. Answers may vary. Possible response: In paragraph three, the author explains how natural disasters and severe weather has affected the Valley of Geysers by providing examples of specific storms and the damage they caused. For instance, the author explains that the typhoon that occurred in October 1981 destroyed some of the geyser; 3. Answers may vary. Possible answer: Volcanic activity may have caused the landslide. In paragraph two, the author explains that geysers occur in volcanic areas; 4. According to paragraph 3, the area where the disaster occurred is in the Ring of Fire, an area with lots of volcanic activity.

Page 119. Activity 2: 1. D; 2. Answers may vary. Possible answer: The author believes that although nature has created some beautiful, inspiring wonders all around the world, nature has also been responsible for destroying some of its own works. When natural disasters occur, they can destroy some of the natural beauty on the Earth permanently; Activity 3: 1. D; 2. Answers will vary. Possible response: According to the text, tourists sometimes throw objects into geysers to see if they will explode, affecting the pressure and water flow and disrupting the geyser. Developers sometimes destroy parts of geysers when they build structures on or near them.

Page 120. 3. Answers may vary. Possible response: The author supports the claim by saying that the scientists are actually working with lawmakers to protect the geysers, showing that they really are committed.

Reading and Writing: Literature

Unit 7—Folklore of the World

Lesson 1—Anansi and the Gub-gub Peas

Page 130. Central Ideas, Key Details, and Summaries: 1. B; 2. Answers will vary. Two possible sentences: "So he begged and begged the watchman to let him have some"; "But Anansi was so pushy that the watchman eventually tied him up in the pea field and allowed him to eat until his belly burst"; 3. Answers will vary. Possible response: It was important for the author to include the detail about the watchman not being able to read because this allowed Anansi to trick the watchman into believing that the master allowed Anansi to eat the peas. Anansi did this by reading the fake letter to the watchman. This relates to the theme of the story because the letter was supposedly from the master stating that Anansi was allowed to eat the peas, which was Anansi's plan all along; 4. C; 5. Answers may vary. Possible response: Lion changes because after pulling his first row of weeds, he decides that the work is too hard. Because of his decision to help Anansi, Lion ends up being hunted by the master. He runs away and must live in the bushes so that he won't be caught.

Page 131. Understanding Figurative Language: 1. hyperbole, B; 2. imagery, B

Page 132. Understanding Personification: 1. B; 2. The golden leaf; Challenge: Lion shook his shiny, golden mane. "Why should I help you? You are a liar, Anansi!" Anansi got

so mad that steam came from his ears. He stomped his feet, but Lion just walked away. A gust of wind blew past, rattling the peas in their shells so that they seemed to be laughing at Anansi.

Lesson 2—Aladdin, the Magic Lamp, and the Princess

Page 135. Central Ideas, Key Details, and Summaries: 1. C; 2. Answers will vary. Possible answer: I would include the detail that Aladdin is tricked by a magician into finding the lamp, and the detail that he gets riches and marries a princess because the genie grants his wishes; 3. It is important for Aladdin to go into the cave and find the lamp instead of the magician because the genie who grants all of Aladdin's wishes is in the lamp. If the magician had gone into the cave and found the lamp instead of Aladdin, then Aladdin would never have had his wishes fulfilled, which is the main action of the story; 4. Answers will vary. Possible answer: The magician gets mad when Aladdin will not give him the lamp and shuts Aladdin in the cave using a rock. Aladdin is worried when he is stuck in the cave, but that is also how he discovers the genie; 5. The sultan's daughter learns that Mestikel only wants to marry her because of all the money that she has. He says, "Why, if she has no money, I certainly do not want to marry her!"

Page 136. Understanding Alliteration: 1. D; 2. Descended, deeper, dense, darkness, depths; 3. Ferocious, fearsome-looking fellow; Challenge: Answers will vary. Possible answer: The mighty, mean magician meant to murder Aladdin.

Page 137. Comparing Media: 1. Answers will vary. Possible answer: The story does not give a lot of information about Mestikel. However, I know he is not a nice person because he only wants to marry the princess for her money and rejects her when he thinks she is poor. I do not like him; 2. Answers will vary. Possible answer: I pictured the magician as a mean man with a sly look on his face. I imagined him talking to Aladdin quietly most of the time but then sometimes yelling when he commands him or loses his temper; 3. Answers will vary. Possible answer: I think the genie scared Aladdin when he appeared from the lamp. I think the genie is big and that he moves around like a cloud.

Page 138. 4. Answers will vary. Possible answer: The video gives more information about Mestikel than the story does. It tells us that he is a coward and does not like to help people, in addition to being greedy and not loving the princess. I did not have a good picture of Mestikel in my mind after reading the story, but the video makes him look mean; 5. Answers will vary. Possible answer: The magician in the video seems nicer at first than the magician in the story, even though he turns out to be bad in both versions. The magician was very tall and bright in the video, which

Answer Key

was different from the older, shorter man that I pictured when I read the story; 6. Answers will vary. Possible answer: The genie is very different in the video from how I pictured him in the story. He has a white pointed hat or cloth on his head and large white gloves, and it is hard to see his face. He does float, like I imagined, but he looks kind of scary.

Unit 8—Greek and Roman Myths
Lesson 1—The Sun Chariot

Page 145. Central Ideas, Key Details, and Summaries: 1. C; 2. Answers may vary but should include at least two of the following elements: the explanation of why the sun moves across the sky, how it always stays in the same path, why there are dried up rivers and areas of the earth like deserts, where lightning bolts come from. Possible response: It explains why the sun appears to move across the sky during the day. According to the myth, the sun is pulled across the sky by the god Helios, who carries it in a chariot pulled by four horses. The myth also explains where the deserts came from by telling how the heat of the out of control chariot burned up the ground and dried up the rivers.

Page 146. Characters and Inferences: 1. Zeus–S, Helios–D, Epaphus–S, Clymene–S, Phaethon–D; 2. Answers will vary depending on student's answer to question #1, but the student should use either Phaethon or Helios. Possible response: Phaethon is one dynamic character in the myth because he changes in the story. At the beginning, he is very proud. He boasts a lot, and thinks he can do the same things that his father can do. Once he gets in trouble in the chariot, though, he realizes that he was wrong and should not have been so prideful. Because he learns a lesson, he is dynamic, even though he dies at the end.

Page 147. 3. B; 4. Answers will vary. Possible response: From reading this myth, I can tell that the Greeks and Romans were very curious and imaginative. When they looked at the world around them, they wanted to know why things worked the way they did, like why the sun moves across the sky and why parts of the earth are very dry and burnt-looking but others are not. When they did not know the answer, they made up very creative stories to explain these things, so I can infer that the Greeks and Romans were both curious and creative; 5. A

Page 149. Making Words: 1. Root: Possible; Prefix im-; Because the word impossible means that something is not possible, the prefix -im means "not."

Page 150. 2. D; 3. Magna–4, root; dis-–5, prefix; gress–2, root; de-–6, prefix; struct–1, root; -ive–3, suffix

Lesson 2—Summer Sun

Page 152. Types of Writing: 1. Poetry; 2. Prose; 3. Answers

will vary. Possible response: Poetry is a style of writing that is very different from prose. Although it does not have to, it often uses rhyming words and has a rhythm when you read it. Prose does not usually use rhyming words and does not have a rhythm. Poetry is also divided into stanzas, while prose is not. Prose usually uses sentences and paragraphs and is more like how we speak, while poetry could be compared to how we sing; 4. B

Page 153. 5. Answers will vary. Possible responses: One theme in "Summer Sun" that is not in "The Sun Chariot" is the happiness that is associated with the sun. The poem describes the light of the sun reaching into dark places and spreading light and joy, by using words like "glad," "smiles," "bright," and "please." The Sun Chariot acknowledges that the sun can be beautiful but is more focused on the things the characters are doing and the bad things that the sun can do, like drying up rivers and making the ground dry out; Understanding Figurative Language: Activity 1: 1. In the poem, "he" is the sun. Robert Louis Stevenson is using personification, the type of figurative language where the writer describes something that is not human with human-like qualities so the reader will understand it. In the first line, he says "Great is the sun, and wide he goes," so it makes sense that "he" is "the sun." "He" is also described as showering rays, having golden fingers and a golden face, and going through the sky, so "he" cannot really be a human and must be something else, like the sun; 2. Answers may vary. Possible explanation: No, "we" is not an example of personification. "We" is referring to people, because the sentence says "we pull" the blinds. Pulling the blinds is something that humans do in this poem, not something that the sun does. Because the action is really being done by humans and not by something that is just being described as a human, it cannot be personification.

Page 154. 3. C; 4. Wording will vary. Possible response: The attic is being personified because the sun makes it "glad." An attic cannot really be "glad," because that is a feeling. Because the attic is being described as having a human feeling, it is being personified; Activity 2: 1. "Golden fingers" is used as a metaphor for sunbeams; 2. The sun is referred to as the "gardener of the World"; meanings will vary. Possible response: I think that the writer is referring to how the sun seems like it takes care of the earth and all the things on it, like a gardener takes care of the garden.

Lesson 3—The Reasons for the Seasons

Page 158. Central Ideas, Key Details, and Summaries: 1. Answers will vary. Possible response: The main idea of this myth is that the difference in the seasons is the result of the harvest goddess Demeter being sad for half of the year because her daughter is in the Underworld and happy for the other half because her daughter is with her; 2. Answers will vary. Possible response: One moral in the myth is that it is better for people who disagree to compromise than for them to stay mad at each other. One of the main problems in the text, Demeter's sadness about not having her daughter and her anger at Hades, is at least partly solved by a compromise. In the myth, if there had not been a compromise, then it would be winter all the time; 3. Answers will vary. Possible response: I can infer that Aphrodite is power-hungry. When she tells Cupid to shoot the love arrow at Hades, she mentions that it will give her some control in the Underworld. Apparently, she is not happy with the amount of power she already has as the goddess of love and wants more.

Page 159. 4. B; 5. D

Pages 160–161. Understanding Denotations and Connotations: 1. Answers will vary. Possible response: Both of the words tell the reader that Demeter is looking for Persephone; The word "scour" is stronger and seems like she is looking harder. Even used in this way, the word has associations of scrubbing very hard, almost like Demeter is "scrubbing" the whole earth to find her daughter; 2. Answers will vary. Possible response: Yes, if the words are moved around, the sentences still make sense and say basically the same thing. This means that the denotations of the words are very similar; "Disappointed" has a slightly different connotation than "unhappy" and "sad." It has the feeling of being excited about something and then being extra sad when it doesn't happen, so it makes sense that the word is used when Demeter gets her hopes up about Persephone coming back and then is sad when it doesn't happen; 3. Answers will vary. Possible response: "Stop!" she cried, "You shouldn't be doing this, Hades!"; "Seeing that her advice had been ignored, and feeling very sorry for Persephone and her mother, Cyane began to sob, and cried so much that she turned into a stream of water"; 4. Cry–to call loudly; shout; yell; Cry–to weep; shed tears, with or without sound.

Page 162. 5. Answers will vary. Possible responses: To call loudly, shout, or yell; Connotations will vary. Possible responses: Call out: Even though these words are used to describe Persephone's actions while she is being kidnapped, they do not have the same strong feelings attached to them than the other two words. Someone who calls out might do so for any reason. The connotations are not really good or bad; Cry: The connotations for this word are stronger than for "call out." To cry something instead of calling it makes it sound more urgent, like maybe there is danger or something wrong. The connotations are mainly bad; Exclaim: This word has connotations that are not as negative as "cry" but still stronger than "call out." It has the feeling of being excited about something, maybe in a good way but maybe not. When Demeter exclaims to Zeus, it is because she is worried and feeling strongly about getting Persephone back.

Stop and Think! Units 7–8 Review

Page 166. Activity 1: 1.Having no occupant; 2. unoccupied; To reject with disfavor, to consider not worthy; 3. To move or act quickly, hurry; 4. To impress favorably, charm; 5. To regard with respect and admiration; 6. Unhappy or miserable, as in feeling, condition, or appearance; 7. Used as an exclamation to express sorrow, grief, pity, concern, or afraid of evil; 8. Not returned.

Page 167. 9. Rushed, ran; 10. Answers will vary. Sample response: Spurn: from looking this word up earlier, I know that this word means the same as reject, but is stronger. It has the connotation of not just rejecting someone but doing it in a very mean way that expresses complete disgust and contempt. These connotations make sense because Narcissus leads Echo to believe that he is interested and then treats her with disgust, which is a terrible way to reject someone; "Reject" still has the negative denotation of telling someone to go away or getting rid of someone, but does not have the same strong connotations of meanness that "spurn" has. "Dismissing" someone means that you are sending them away, but it is not as strong as rejecting and definitely not as strong as spurning. It carries the connotation of the person just not caring about someone and not thinking they are important, rather than trying to get rid of them in a way that is mean, like "spurn."

Page 168. Activity 2: 1. D; 2. A-3; B-1; C-5; D-2; E-4.

Stop and Think! Units 7–8 Understand

Page 169. Activity 1: 1. Narcissus is a static character. Explanations may vary. Possible explanation: Narcissus is a static character because static characters do not change and grow during a story and neither does Narcissus. He is vain at the beginning of the story, and it is his vanity that ends up killing him at the end of the story; 2. C; 3. Answers may vary. Possible explanation: The story explains why sounds echo in the forests and mountains. According to the myth, it is because Echo, who can only repeat what other people say, stayed in the woods and mountains after Narcissus rejected her. Her body has faded away and only her voice remains; 4. Answers may vary. Possible answer: I can infer that Narcissus' body turned into the flower that the nymphs found.

Page 170. 5. B; 6. Answers may vary. Possible answer: One of the people who Narcissus rejected prays to the gods, so the gods trap Narcissus into falling in love with his own reflection. He is so in love with his reflection that he stays by the pond all the time and no longer treats other people badly; 7. Answers may vary. Possible answer: Yes, Narcissus' death could have been avoided if people had remembered the prophesy from his birth and made sure he never saw his reflection in the water. According to the prophesy, if he never saw his reflection he would live a full life, but the people forgot about the prophesy until it was too late; 8. A

Unit 9—Poetry

Lesson 1—Echoing Green

Page 176. Central Ideas, Key Details, and Summaries: 1. Answers may vary. Possible answer: In "Echoing Green," William Blake describes a spring day—the beautiful birds singing, the sun shining, and cheerful children playing in the green grass. The poet also describes the old man sitting under a tree thinking about when he was a child playing with his friends and realizing that spring doesn't last forever. By the third stanza, the sun is setting, the children are tired and going home to sleep; 2. D; 3. Answers may vary. Possible answer: In the first stanza, the poet describes bells ringing and birds singing to welcome the spring. In the second stanza, people young and old are described enjoying the spring day as well.

Page 177. Analyzing Structure: 1. Answers may vary. Possible answer: The organization of the poem in three stanzas suggests that the poem has three parts; the beginning of the spring day (in the morning when the sun is rising and children are going outside to play), the middle in the second stanza (in the afternoon when the old man is remembering his childhood friends and playing with them on the green grass), and the end of the day in the third stanza (when the sun is setting, the birds are in their nests, and the children are going home).

Page 179. Word Choice and Tone: 1. Stanza 1: The sun does arise-5; And make happy the skies-6; The merry bells ring-5; To welcome the spring-5; The skylark and thrush-5; The birds of the bush-5; Sing louder around-5; To the bells' cheerful sound-6; While our sports shall be seen-6; On the echoing green.-6; Stanza 3: Till the little ones weary-7; No more can be merry-6; The sun does descend-5; And our sports have an end-6; Round the laps of their mother-7; Many sisters and brothers-7; Like birds in their nest-5; Are ready for rest-5; And sport no more seen-5; On the darkening green-6; 2. Answers will vary. Possible response: The third stanza has more six and seven syllable lines, whereas the first stanza has more five syllable lines. The first stanza is more upbeat and fast because of fewer syllables. The third stanza is longer and drawn out, which creates a more tired feeling; 3. Answers will vary. Possible response: The poet also uses rhyming words to set the rhythm of the poem. An example is: The skylark and thrush, / The birds of the bush; 4. C

Page 180. Understanding Figurative Language: 1. Yes, the poem has similes. Possible example: Many sisters and brothers, / Like birds in their nest, / Are ready for rest; 2. A. Positive; B. Negative; C. Positive; D. Positive; E. Negative

Page 181. Understanding Personification: 1. Answers may vary. Possible response: The sun does arise, / And make happy the skies; 2. Answers will vary. Possible answer: The personification of the sun, the bells, and the birds in the first part of the poem add happiness and joy to the beginning of the poem that creates contrast with the more quiet and less joyful ending that signals the end of the day.

Lesson 2—The Owl and the Pussycat

Page 183. Analyzing Structure: 1. Kitty said to the Owl, "You elegant fowl, (a) / How charmingly sweet you sing! (b) / Oh! let us be married; too long we have tarried, (c) / But what shall we do for a ring?" (b) / They sailed away, for a year and a day, (a) / To the land where the bong-tree grows; (b) / And there in a wood a Piggy-wig stood, (c) / With a ring at the end of his nose, (b) / His nose, (b)/ His nose, (b)/ With a ring at the end of his nose (b); 2. They find a wedding ring; 3. Answers may vary. Possible answer: The poet includes this stanza in the poem because it explains why the cat and owl decide to get married and how they came to find a wedding ring. This fits into the overall poem because in the first stanza, the cat and owl are traveling together, and the owl falls in love with the cat. In the third stanza, they buy a ring and finally get married. The poem as a whole explains the cat and owl's silly journey and how they fall in love and get married.

Page 184. 1. Stanza 1: What a beautiful Kitty you are, / You are, / You are! / What a beautiful Kitty you are!; Stanza 2: With a ring at the end of his nose, / His nose, / His nose, / With a ring at the end of his nose; Stanza 3: They danced by the light of the moon, / The moon, / The moon, / They danced by the light of the moon; 2. Answers may vary. Possible answer: The refrains at the end of each stanza help to create an upbeat, fun, silly song-like feel and tone because of the repetition of the same phrases at the end of each stanza. Because the owl is singing to the cat throughout the poem, it makes sense that the refrains make the entire poem feel like a song.

Page 185. Comparing Media: 1. Answers may vary. Possible answer: The narrator in the video recites the poem very carefully, not too slow and not too fast; 2. Answers may vary. Possible answer: Based on the video, the tone of the poem is upbeat and silly. It feels like a song; 3. Answers may vary. Possible answer: Seeing the owl and the pussycat helps to get a better picture of what the poet is describing in the poem. The characters in the video bring the poem to life and make the events in the poem seem more lifelike; 4. Answers are personal to the student experience and will vary; 5. Answers are personal to the student experience and will vary.

Stop and Think! Unit 9 Review

Page 189. Activity 1: 1. In "The Wind's Visit," Dickinson uses similes. A simile is comparing two unlike things with the words like or as. Dickinson also uses personification, which is giving non-human things human characteristics such as talking; 2. Answers may vary. Possible answer: An example of a simile from the poem is: The wind tapped like a tired man. An example of a personification from the poem is: His countenance a billow; 3. Answers may vary. Possible answer: The author compares the wind to a man, which gives the reader the sense that the wind is like a visitor stopping by to say hello or check in. This helps to express the poem's theme, which is that the narrator is lonely before the wind stops by, enjoys the wind's company, and then feels lonely again when the wind leaves. The use of personification in the poem helps the author express the friendly nature of her relationship with the wind. The wind is like an old friend whose voice is like music; he brings joy when he visits and leaves emptiness when he leaves.

Page 190. 4. Answers may vary. Possible answer: Example of my own simile: She dashed through the bushes like a cheetah chasing its prey across the plains. Example of my own personification: The trees danced elegantly across the night sky, with the stars singing joyfully behind them; 5. A; Challenge: Answers will vary widely, but should include three stanzas, each with at least four lines in the quatrain style with A/B/C/B rhyme scheme. The poem should also include at least one example of figurative language, such as a simile or personification.

Stop and Think! Unit 9 Understand

Page 191. Activity 1: 1. Answers may vary. Possible answer: The narrator is at home alone and hears tapping at the door. When she opens the door, it is the wind. The wind is fast even though he doesn't have feet, and when he speaks, its like music or humming birds singing. The narrator cannot offer him a seat because he is moving so fast. While the narrator enjoys their visit together, it is very short, and when the wind leaves, the narrator feels alone; 2. Answers may vary. Possible answer: The poem explains that the wind is like an old friend whose visit is very short. Before the wind arrives, the narrator is alone in the house, and after the wind leaves, the narrator becomes lonely. This supports the poem's central theme of loneliness; 3. Answers may vary. Possible answer: At the beginning of the poem, the narrator says: The wind tapped like a tired man, / And like a host, "Come in," / I boldly answered. This shows her excitement to have the wind as a visitor. At the end of the poem, she says: He visited, still flitting; / Then, like a timid man, / Again he tapped—'t was flurriedly— / And I became alone. This shows her sadness and loneliness, and it indicates that the visit was very brief; 4. D

Page 192. Activity 2: 1. A; 2. The narrator in the poem seems to be the author. She is the one who welcomes the wind into her home. In the first stanza, she states: The wind tapped like a tired man, / And like a host, "Come in," / I boldly answered; entered then / My residence within; 3. The narrator's description of the wind at the beginning of the poem is similar to how she describes him at the end. In both places, the wind is like a shy old man knocking at the door. In both the beginning and the end, the narrator repeats that the wind "tapped" like a tired or timid man; Activity 3: 1. In the second stanza, the narrator says the following about the wind: A rapid, footless guest, / To offer whom a chair / Were as impossible as hand / A sofa to the air. This stanza contributes to the theme of a visiting friend who helps the author not feel lonely by calling the wind a guest; 2. D

Page 193. 3. His countenance a billow, (a); His fingers, if he pass, (b); Let go a music, as of tunes (c); Blown tremulous in glass. (b); 4. Yes, the rhyme pattern throughout the poem is the same. In each stanza, there are four lines. The second and fourth lines of each stanza rhyme; 5. The narrator used the word "tapped" at the beginning and the end of the poem to show that the visitor came alone and left alone after a brief visit. The word "tapped" signals the beginning of the wind's visit and when the wind leaves. After the wind leaves, the narrator becomes alone, which contributes to the theme of loneliness in the poem.

GRADES 2–6
TEST PRACTICE
for Common Core

With Common Core Standards being implemented across America, it's important to give students, teachers, and parents the tools they need to achieve success. That's why Barron's has created the *Core Focus* series. These multi-faceted, grade-specific workbooks are designed for self-study learning, and the units in each book are divided into thematic lessons that include:

- Specific, focused practice through a variety of exercises, including multiple-choice, short answer, and extended response questions

- A unique scaffolded layout that organizes questions in a way that challenges students to apply the standards in multiple formats

- "Fast Fact" boxes and a cumulative assessment in Mathematics and English Language Arts (ELA) to help students increase knowledge and demonstrate understanding across the standards

Perfect for in-school or at-home study, these engaging and versatile workbooks will help students meet and exceed the expectations of the Common Core.

Grade 2 Test Practice for Common Core
Maryrose Walsh and Judith Brendel
ISBN 978-1-4380-0550-8
Paperback, $14.99, *Can$16.99*

Grade 3 Test Practice for Common Core
Renee Snyder, M.A. and Susan M. Signet, M.A.
ISBN 978-1-4380-0551-5
Paperback, $14.99, *Can$16.99*

Grade 4 Test Practice for Common Core
Kelli Dolan and Shephali Chokshi-Fox
ISBN 978-1-4380-0515-7
Paperback, $14.99, *Can$16.99*

Grade 5 Test Practice for Common Core
Lisa M. Hall and Sheila Frye
ISBN 978-1-4380-0595-9
Paperback, $14.99, *Can$16.99*

Grade 6 Test Practice for Common Core
Christine R. Gray and Carrie Meyers-Herron
ISBN 978-1-4380-0592-8
Paperback, $14.99, *Can$16.99*

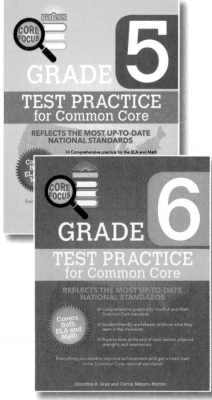

Barron's Educational Series, Inc.
250 Wireless Blvd.
Hauppauge, N.Y. 11788
Order toll-free: 1-800-645-3476

In Canada:
Georgetown Book Warehouse
34 Armstrong Ave.
Georgetown, Ontario L7G 4R9
Canadian orders: 1-800-247-7160

Prices subject to change without notice.

Coming soon to your local book store or visit **www.barronseduc.com**

(#295 R11/14)